# D.C
## UNMASKED & *Undressed*

## A MEMOIR

# D.C. UNMASKED & *Undressed*

## A MEMOIR

LILLIAN McEWEN

A MEMOIR

Copyright © 2011 Lillian McEwen

TitleTown Publishing, LLC
P.O. Box 12093  Green Bay, WI  54307-12093
920.737.8051 | titletownpublishing.com

Edited by Katie Vecchio
Cover design by Mandy Kain
Interior layout and design by Erika L. Block
Sketches by Lillian McEwen | Photographed by Thomas G. Marx

PUBLISHER'S CATALOGING-IN-PUBLICATION DATA:

McEwen, Lillian.
D.C. unmasked & undressed : a memoir / Lillian McEwen. -- 1st ed.
Green Bay, WI : TitleTown Pub., c2011.

p. ; cm.

ISBN: 978-0-9820009-9-1
1. McEwen, Lillian. 2. Lawyers--Washington (D.C.)--Biography.
3. African Americans--Biography. 4.Washington (D.C.)--Politics
and Government. 5. Thomas, Clarence, 1948- 6. Child abuse. 7. Sexual
Freedom--Washington. (D.C.) 8. Racially Mixed Women--Biography. I. Title.

KF373.M3984 A3 2011
340.092--dc22 1101

Printed in the USA by Thomson-Shore
first edition ♻ printed on recycled paper
10 9 8 7 6 5 4 3 2 1

This book is dedicated to my daughter,
Velma Michelle McEwen,
who is better than me in every way.

# CONTENTS

# Acknowledgments

The process of writing has shown me how much I owe to others. The sacrifice of my two oldest siblings enabled me to survive my childhood. A middle-aged coworker demonstrated how to act bravely in the face of danger. My daughter forced me to love for the first time. And a loving friend helped me to stay at a difficult job for more than ten years so that I could earn a pension.

I am grateful for the support and encouragement of my family in this endeavor, especially of Mitch, Al, Butch, Mike, Pat and Cameron. I am also grateful for the patience and good will of my friends, especially Theresa, Renee, Jamala, William, Andrae, Ken, Bob, and Charles. Members of the National Bar Association, the Washington Bar Association, and my memoir class in Provincetown are also thanked, for their acts of kindness.

My story might not have emerged in its present form without the Norman Mailer Foundation and Kaylie Jones. Finally, thank you, Tracy Ertl of Title-Town Publishing for leaping off this cliff with me.

# Preface

A memoir rather than an autobiography, this book omits what some might consider important facts. It omits my parents' names, the date of my birth, and a strict time line. These omissions are intentional. My intent is to describe experiences of significance to me. Their significance reflects the power that the events exerted to shape my interior life and my future. I hope that this book performs in some small measure the miracle that reading has worked for me – revealing what lies behind the mask that we all don at some point.

It is the revelation or unmasking of truth that I seek here, a truth that transcends facts and that emerges from a fearless examination and exposition of the past and of pivotal thought processes. For me, this effort is so difficult that it must be accomplished indirectly, by the description of scenes that intense reflection forces to the surface of awareness and then to a page. The scenes illuminate the fears, turning points, characters, and actions of my life. These strands are woven to create my unique tapestry. This memoir tells a true story. I have changed the names and identifying characteristics of some persons in the story, however, in an effort to preserve their privacy.

# *Introduction*

*D.C. Unmasked & Undressed* is a memoir. It can be summarized as: Girl from dysfunctional family meets boy from same; his name is Clarence Thomas. This story of my life includes events, characters, and insights related to my miserable childhood, my legal career, and my varied sexual adventures. It is the culmination of pressure from many friends and family members who wanted me to write it. *D.C. Unmasked & Undressed* is not chronological, but is organized around short life stories that are important to me.

President Obama would describe me as a mutt, as he candidly described himself. Like him, I am the product of a racially mixed marriage. I suffered in a dysfunctional family and then persisted in a disappointing marriage for more than ten years. My journey from a department-store cashier to technical copy editor to counsel to the United States Senate Judiciary Committee caused me to work for then-Senator Joseph Biden when I was thirty-five years old. I worked on speeches, legal memoranda, and committee reports. I investigated judicial nominees and I organized hearings. Later, as an attorney in private practice, I represented murderers, rapists, armed robbers, and drug dealers—the same types of men and women whom I had prosecuted as an assistant United States attorney in my first job out of law school. My journey eventually took me to the United States Securities and Exchange Commission, where I was a federal administrative law judge for more than ten years.

I worked hard and played hard, too. Along the way and for several years, I was the not-so-secret lover of a sitting Supreme Court Justice who has recently published his own memoir.

# Scene One

## Never Too Late

I was in my bedroom, upstairs in the attic. The bitter pills were ready, in the bottle. I had thought about it too long. I spilled the aspirin tablets onto the narrow, single bed that filled the room and, slowly, I counted them out. About eighty tablets—white and powerful—were ready for me to swallow them. I had no reason to hesitate. Life was mine to take and nobody had power over me anymore. They never should have had it, anyway. But, incessantly, my parents had said that my seven siblings and I should never have been born. No friend cared about me. No one ever had.

The men I knew were not my friends, although some of them wanted to marry me. That was not enough. In the pit of my stomach, the loneliness and disappointment were painful, but physical pain was nothing compared to the vision I had of my life, a future filled with more ridicule from my neighbors and more hostility from my coworkers and fellow college students. I reached for the bottle, which had a few pills left in it. I shook them out onto the blanket.

My Uncle Eddie had built the attic room when I was about eight years old. Even then, eleven years earlier, I knew that he was an alcoholic, with his bloodshot eyes, slurred speech, and crooked smiles. His long, floppy hair was coal black, falling rakishly over one perfectly arched eyebrow, and he was wiry, funny, and the most beautiful light-skinned man I had ever seen. My brother Tony looked just like him. When Eddie finished transforming the unused attic into three bedrooms—stifling hot in the summer and unheated and freezing in the winter—my mother kicked him out of the house. I never saw him again, except posing with a mischievous grin on his face and a hand on his hip in old black-and-white photographs with scalloped edges.

I swallowed ten of the aspirin and tried to gulp down another handful with several ounces of water, but I couldn't do it. They were too bitter and they stuck in my throat. I had to cough them back up. Then, the tears began.

When I was ten years old, I had vowed never to smile again and never to cry again. I would never smile again because, if I did, people might think I was happy, and I knew I was not. They also might think I was smiling in order to please them, and I never wanted to fall into that trap. It certainly was not possible to please my mother; I had watched as my older sister and brother had tried it and as my mother had destroyed both of them. Of course, I eventually lost the battle of the smiles. There was too much pleasure to be taken from men and music, too many wonderful endings in books, and too much irony in my life. I had to smile at the jokes that the world had already played on me.

But I had not lost the battle of the tears, until I sat on my bed with the aspirin. When I fell down the basement stairs four years earlier, I did not cry, even though everybody in the emergency room thought I had broken my arm. When I scalded my left arm with boiling oatmeal, I did not cry, even though the five-inch scar from the second-degree burn was still visible eight years later. And I had not cried when my brother Tony had smashed my hand in the kitchen door and blood squirted from my fingertip that had to be stitched up. I had not cried when my mother whipped me, even when she drew blood with the leather belt that had been burned on the tip.

As I forced the second batch of acid-tasting pills down my throat, sobs wracked my body. In waves of self-pity, I cried for myself. Then I cried for my sister and my brother and I felt the familiar rage against my mother, who had kicked them and whipped them with rope, tree branches, belts, and extension cords until she perspired.

Ten years of swallowed tears finally ran down my cheeks and

my tears and my rage somehow saved me. In a kind of trance that lasted about an hour, I gazed at the remaining pills. "Maybe I should try the razor again," I thought. But, the year before, after a few superficial cuts, the sight of my own blood had stopped me from accomplishing the act.

Now, rage stopped me—rage against a world that teased me because I talked, looked, dressed, and acted differently, rage against a neighborhood that would not accept me, and rage against a family that forced me to turn to strangers. Fine, strangers could become friends and friends could become family. It is never too late to have a happy childhood. I had nothing to prove to the world, and crying was allowed. I had just proven that. I finished crying, emerged from my trance and heaved a great sigh of relief. I vowed that I would make the next part of my life different and better. I picked up the water bottle, the aspirin, and the aspirin bottle, threw them in the trash, and walked out of the house. That was my last suicide attempt. I kept it a secret, like the scars on my left wrist, to stroke like an old rosary in times of stress.

*My mother before the marriage.*

# Scene Two

## The Meeting

My mother was fifteen years old when they met. She had come to the park so that she could finish her homework in peace. With twelve brothers and sisters sharing the big frame house, life on the farm had been hectic. She seldom saw her father, who preferred to live close to his construction business in Hansom, Virginia.

In Virginia, my mother had never seen anyone like the man in the park. As she bent over the book in her lap, she peered at him from the corner of her eye. This was not the first time she had noticed him. She wondered what her Aunt Jessie and her Aunt Frances and her young cousins would think of him. They had been happy to take her in when she decided to leave the farm, the outhouse, and the backyard pump to accompany them to Washington, D.C., but they would not be happy to meet the man in the park.

He walked toward her. She raised her head from the book and a bright smile lit up his handsome face as he doffed his hat to her. It was 1935, and men who could afford them never went out in public without a hat or a cap. But his hat was special—a fedora, with a small fluffy feather that perfectly matched the color of his three-piece suit and soft leather shoes. The feather swayed in the breeze that his extravagant gesture created.

He was special, too. His raised hat revealed polished, wavy hair that fell to one side of his face, just like her brother Eddie's. As the man darted to sit on the park bench before she could escape, my mother noticed that his slanted eyes, sharp nose, thin moustache, and full lips made him look like a much older version of her youngest brother. They both looked like the movie star, Clark Gable. Every woman in America loved Clark Gable.

Smiling back at him, she wondered what love was really like. She thought he was probably rich and wondered if she was too young for him.

5

She decided not to tell the handsome man her true age.

My father was thirty-eight years old. As he raised his new hat in greeting, he decided to overcome his natural shyness and talk to the young girl on the bench, who appeared to be Filipina or Cuban. He hoped that she would not escape before he lost his courage. It had taken him weeks to find a fedora that matched the three-piece suit and shoes, which had cost his entire paycheck from the Library of Congress the month before.

My father hurried to get closer as my mother glanced up from the book in her lap, and he was struck again by the fact that she looked like the family of Anna, the daughter he had left behind, in Cuba, ten years earlier. She had the same long, chestnut hair, slanted eyes, high cheekbones, and square jaw.

Grief for his deceased wife made him hesitate as he approached the wooden bench. His beloved wife had died of pneumonia, so suddenly that it had caused him to leave Cuba in a panic—the same kind of panic that compelled him to leave his birth family in the Philippines twenty years before. As he ran toward the beautiful girl, he assured himself once again that his daughter was better off without him. He could not have raised her alone, and her maternal grandmother in Cuba was ecstatic when he gave her permission to keep the toddler whom she doted on.

A dozen Filipinas worked in his offices and he got along with them, but the only woman in America who fascinated him was the one in front of him, the woman who had finally looked up and stared at him directly. Many times over the past year, he had admired her in the park. Now, it was late spring and her short-sleeved, thin, cotton dress clung with sweat to her tiny waist and voluptuous breasts and hips. His artist's keen eye had stripped her naked countless times and he had already fallen in love with her body. But how old was she? She smiled broadly at him with a puzzled expression on her face. He estimated that she was probably a college student. Was he too old for her? He decided not to tell the beautiful woman his true age.

6

# Scene Three

Catholic School

It was too late. The nun had seen me reading the book before I could hide it beneath the chair, and she was marching resolutely toward me to escort me from the auditorium, where the assembly had already begun. Wondering what was in the book that had been snatched from my trembling arms—and why I had been reading it instead of paying attention to the  assembly speakers, as we had been ordered to do—the entire population of Saint Martin's Catholic School watched as Sister Mary Patrick forcefully propelled me to the nearest exit. Even though I was just in the fourth grade, I knew that I was lucky to be in the school at  all, and graduation from the eighth grade seemed an eternity away.

Hurrying to Mother Superior's office, I noticed the heavy wooden beads that encircled the waist of the nun beside me. The beads ended in a crucifix that banged against her shins when she walked. All of the nuns fingered their beads in a constant state of agitation or piety.

As we walked, I examined Sister Mary Patrick's vestments. She was a sister of the order of Notre Dame and only her hands and face revealed her to be a white woman. Her head and hair were covered by a tight linen cap and a veil that fell past her waist to form a V down her back. The white starched cap emerged from around her ears and covered her forehead and the sides of her face, shielding her profile from view. A starched white collar pinched her chin and ran in a fan to  her waist, concealing her shoulders and chest like a suit of armor. Underneath this carapace, a black, long-sleeved woolen dress with a voluminous skirt hid the body beneath it from her neck to the tops of her shoes. Her ankles were covered in thick black stockings under black, laced oxfords with one-inch heels. I considered this black and white ensemble to be the most gorgeous outfit in the world. Although I had been enrolled in the school for only two years, I knew that I wanted to be a nun, living in the convent across the playground from the school and walking six blocks to church where the priests said Mass every day.

When I was in the second grade, my parents had transferred all the younger children to Saint Martin's School, never bothering to tell us why. The girls wore navy-blue jumper uniforms with white blouses and navy-blue bows. The boys wore navy-blue pants, white shirts, and navy-blue neckties. My classroom included fifty-four students, arranged alphabetically with the girls on one side of the room and the boys on the other.

The nuns maintained discipline by generating a series of signals on the clicker, two pieces of wood struck against each other by means of a rubber band. Priests and enthusiastic nuns administered further discipline by banging rulers against fingers and by wielding paddles in the cloak room. Memorization was the principal teaching method, and they taught catechism and liturgical music daily. The Mass consisted of Latin prayers, and most of the music was also in Latin.

Although I desperately wanted to enter this orderly, spiritual world, I engaged in one activity that I could not sacrifice, and that was reading. In my family, reading required walking to the public library on Ninth Street, checking out as many books as we could carry, and walking back home—about a mile each way. As soon as I could walk, I made these trips with my siblings. I must have taught myself to read, since I have no recollection of being read to and do not recall a time when I was unable to read.

By the time I had reached the fourth grade, I had exhausted the children's section at the library, and I made lists so that my older brother Tony, who was in high school, could borrow books for me to read. These books became my parents, teachers, friends, and escape. I took them everywhere and seized every opportunity to read them. I had already spent one sleepless night reading half of the book that now lay open on Mother

Superior's desk, and I desperately hoped she would not confiscate it, as I expected to finish it that night.

Her face softened into a slight smile. She pushed the book aside and reached to open a desk drawer. I flinched, but she pulled out a box of chocolates and offered it to me. "Take one, child," she insisted. It looked like the box of Whitman's Samplers that my mother brought home from her trysts. Sometimes, she gave us the pieces that she had tasted and rejected. Most of the time, those pieces were caramel, which I had already grown to despise. My abject terror had to be obvious and I knew that Mother Superior was trying to be nice to me and get me to calm down, but the proffer had the opposite effect. I took a small bite from the round confection in my hand. Uh oh! It was a dark-chocolate covered whole cherry with syrup in the middle. The nibble released a torrent of salty-sweet liquid that erupted over my lips, chin, and blouse. I choked down the rest of the  piece so that more liquid would not spill out.

The nun asked me a question. "Where did you get this book from, child?" My eyes swelled with tears from humiliation, fear, and the candied obstruction in my throat. "From my older brother," I mumbled. "He is in high school. I write down  the titles and authors and he borrows them for me."

Mother Superior had never met my brother but surely she knew that ours was the first black family admitted to the school, which was still racially segregated. All the other black Catholic students were required to attend a different Catholic school, Holy Redeemer, several blocks away. In that school, the priests and nuns were also black. Saint Martin's didn't have any black priests, nuns, or students—besides us—and it would be several years before they would admit additional black students. In my confused state, I neither heard nor understood what the nun said next. All I knew was that I  was glad to get the book back in my arms and, as I scurried to my classroom, I was relieved that I had not  been punished. The book was *Uncle Tom's Cabin.*

Soon, my book lists gave way to author lists as I developed preferences. Dostoevsky, Tolstoy, Zola, Pushkin, Dumas, Flaubert, Joyce, Dickens, Shakespeare, Rand, Nin, Shaw, James, Melville, Mailer, and Poe became my favorite companions, in no particular order. By the time I graduated from Saint Martin's, I had lost my faith and, along with it, my desire to be a nun. My literary companions helped me to escape and to make sense of my world, filled as it was with adult issues like abortion, teen pregnancy, child abuse, and violence. The Catholic church and the liturgy were of no assistance and, in my great effort to define my own life, I abandoned them.

When I was nineteen years old, a book that I happened to be reading had a great effect on my life. Riding on a bus in the sweltering Washington, D.C. summertime, I was on my way to work in the morning when I saw Walter standing nearby. Walter and I had attended the same high school and he was home from Amherst for the summer. He struck up a conversation with me. "What are you reading?" he asked, pointing to the book in my lap. I have always been prone to motion sickness and I was unable to read on the bus without feeling its effects, but I carried a book to read while waiting for the bus to arrive. I gave him my telephone number and, the next day, I was pleasantly surprised when he called to invite me to a Georgetown house party, given by a college chum. We had barely spoken in high school, where he was a year ahead of me, and he was attending an Ivy League men's school, while I was merely at the local teacher's college.

About two years after that chance meeting on the bus, we were married. Years later, discussing the encounter, I asked why he had asked me for my number and called me. "I decided to get to know you better when I saw the title of the book in your lap," he explained. "Your finger held a place that was more than halfway through it. Do you remember the title of the book you were reading that day?" he asked, grinning. I wracked my brain. "I don't even recall having a book in my lap," I was ashamed to admit. "It was such a habit, though, that I'm sure that I did have a book." He grinned some more. "Lillian," he said, "I remember the title well. It was *War and Peace*. I still don't know anybody else who has actually read that book. That's why I asked for your number and called you."

# Scene Four
## You Think You Cute

"You think you cute." I heard the gang of uniformed school girls running behind me as I walked home from school. Some of them, like me, were in the sixth grade at Saint Martin's Catholic School. Most were in the eighth grade. It had been a terrible week on the playground, and somebody mentioned that they would be looking for me on Friday after school. I had forgotten about the warning and, before I knew it, I was trapped. I had been teased all week about my new hairstyle. On Monday, I had worn my hair unbraided for the first time that year. My thick, wavy hair fell below my shoulders and I could feel it moving across my back when I walked. "She talk like she white," I heard. "Yeah, she think she cute," teased the closest girl.

They would never say that if they only knew how much I hated my hair. It would not hold a press. If I straightened it with an iron comb that was too hot, my hair got burned to a crisp. If I straightened it correctly, the slightest humidity or perspiration caused it to revert to its naturally bushy state. Why couldn't I have beady, kinky hair so that it could be pressed bone straight and stay that way until it was washed? Or why couldn't it be white hair that would lie flat on my head? My hair was too bushy, too thick, and impossible to comb. Hadn't I heard that over and over again from my mother and my older sister? They were both lighter than me, with silky, thin hair that would not hold a curl, and they had both given up on my woolly mane years before. Left to my own devices, all I could manage were two thick braids on either side of my round face. About twice a year, I wore my hair out of the braids, and I was about to be punished for it.

Although I regularly fought with my brothers and sisters, I had never been in a physical altercation with anyone outside my family, and I saw no reason to fight that day. At home, our fights resembled fencing, with complex rules determining how many times a broom or mop could be smashed over the head or shoulders of the opponent, and how long a person could be locked in the basement or bathroom. But there were no rules for the street, and I was outnumbered eight to one. Fighting back was not an option, and I had no brooms or mops for defense. I would just have to walk as fast as I could and hope that they would tire of the one-sided teasing. Surely they had noticed that I had been ignoring them quite effectively all week. One of the group had pulled my hair at recess that day, and another girl had knocked me down onto the cinder-covered playground dust the day before.

"You think you cute, high yellow, don't you?" shouted the biggest, darkest girl, as she ran in front of me. She stopped and planted both fists on her hips as she pushed her face toward me. Suddenly, she stepped forward and shoved me in my bony chest with two fleshy hands. I staggered backwards and looked around for help. It was three-thirty PM, and pedestrians and vehicular traffic usually populated the area. Out of the corner of my eye, I spied a familiar figure turning the corner. It was my older brother. "Junior!" I shouted. "Junior!" I was saved! My big brother would rescue me. I flashed a rare smile.

Junior looked toward me and saw that I was surrounded by a circle of eight girls. Older than me by two years, he was taller and more muscular than any of them. He was named after Daddy and he was my father's favorite, but he was still required to go to the grocery store with me every evening and to help with the dishes each night. When Junior saw the gang, all he could think of was how embarrassing it would be to get beaten up by girls. The risk was too great. "See you later!" he shouted back at me as he ran off in the opposite direction. Some of the girls felt sorry for me and others thought he had run for assistance, so the gang dispersed after a few more half-hearted shoves for good measure. I ran home. When I found Junior, I just looked at him. "I don't fight girls," he explained, feigning chivalry.

14

I was seven years old, sitting on the toilet seat with the lid down. My eyes were clenched shut as I rocked back and forth and hugged myself for comfort. My siblings and I were allowed to lock the doors to both bathrooms inside the four-story house, and I had taken refuge in the larger one. The floor was covered with half-inch hexagonal white tiles that were edged in black. We all bathed in the six-foot long white tub with claw feet and turned squeaky faucets to fill it. A giant red rubber stopper on a rusty chain waited on the edge of the tub to perform its task. But I was not here to bathe, and my privacy would not last long. I forced myself to stop gazing at the two cracked tiles between my feet and concentrated instead on the rusty edge of the mirror clamped to the wall above the porcelain sink, as the five words that had brought me to the bathroom pounded in my head.

She does not love me. She does not love me. How could she not love me? I was not the most beautiful of her five children—my sister Chee Chee was—but I always told on them when they did something wrong. Chee Chee and my brother Tony were both smarter than me, but I did not argue with her the way they did and, still, during that week, she had whipped me nearly as much as she had whipped them. My legs were still covered with large red welts. I massaged the bloody raised streaks as I attempted to absorb the fact that had been proven to me clearly several times over the past week. My options were limited. I resolved as I sat on the toilet to melt into the walls even more. Invisibility would save me, and I would perfect the technique that I had been toying with over the past month. I would say nothing to my mother or my father, and I would break my silence only when forced to do so. Mama did not love me, but I would survive.

As my childhood years crawled by, I had changed cloth diapers and emptied them until my stomach heaved. It had become my responsibility to starch and iron all the cotton shirts and blouses for the school uniforms. This I accomplished with all the efficiency of an accomplished laundry service. I dug splinters from my siblings' feet and elbows with the detachment of a surgeon. I walked to and from the store a mile away, carrying ten peoples' groceries in brown paper bags that I rolled up to use as curlers, which I put in my mother's waist-length hair. Standing behind her comfortable chair, I scratched her dandruff and combed her hair until my knees buckled from exhaustion. Every morning, I cooked bubbly oatmeal, served it to my siblings, and struggled not to vomit at the odor, which I despised. And I suffered as I watched my two older siblings being driven slowly to the brink of insanity that they eventually called schizophrenia. All this I performed in one-sided silences so profound that my voice cracked and broke on the rare occasions when I was compelled to speak in my childhood home.

As the years passed, melting into the walls turned me into a watcher. My stoic silences lasted for days and my family began to describe me as shy. My mother called me by the names of my two sisters, even though I was named after her. Sometimes she did not catch her mistake, and I never bothered to correct her. My two sisters were the troublemakers. Both of them got pregnant as young teenagers and went on to marry abusive spouses. My older sister survived about a dozen suicide attempts that punctuated stays in a mental institution. The regular beatings also took their toll on my oldest brother, Tony, who became a wanderer, speaking gibberish in tongues, living in shelters, and eating from trash bins.

But I am a survivor, I thought, as I sat on the toilet seat lid in my own bathroom at age twenty-three. I did not need to melt into the walls here. I could discard my old bag of tricks. Once again, I had locked the door for privacy. For an entire week, I had not uttered a word to my husband Walter, and he was suffering. During the week, I had snatched periods of solitude and concluded that my silence had to end as soon as possible. Within fifteen minutes of that resolution the day before, Walter had said something to make me angry all over again and the wall went back up. When I emerged from the bathroom, I saw that Walter was in the living room, watching television as usual. Why did he watch television so much? When was the last time he read a book that was not science fiction? As I made my way silently into the kitchen, the man who loved me tried once more to break down the wall. "What can I do to apologize?" he said. Unlike my parents, Walter wanted to do something to make me happy, and he needed me. Didn't he know that I just wanted to be left alone? Hadn't two years of marriage taught him that his apology would just make me angry all over again?

In a rage, I turned away from the kitchen counter to face him. When he fell to the floor and collapsed, I watched as blood trickled from his temple. A twenty-ounce glass bottle of baby oil lay unbroken beside him on the brown shag carpet that I detested. I had hurled the thick bottle at him without even realizing that I had picked it up from the counter. Was he dead? This was the third time I had thrown an object at Walter in anger, but it was the first time that I had struck him in the head.

When I leaned over him and wiped the blood with my sleeve, he did not seem to be breathing. But he was merely unconscious. In a few seconds he opened his eyes. "What happened?" he whispered. As I knelt beside my husband, I promised him and myself that I would not throw anything at him again and that I would abandon the silent treatment and try to tear down the old walls. They had saved me in the past, but they were not working in the new present. He kissed me and forgave me.

*My parents, newly wed in 1937.*

# Scene Six
## What I Want

My childhood was quite miserable before I entered puberty. When I was very young, I thought it could not get any worse, but it did. When I was four years old, my smiling mother told me that she was pregnant and that she would soon give birth to my baby brother or sister. I burst into tears, sobbed uncontrollably, and ran from her and out of the room. I was the fourth child, with an older sister and two older brothers who tried to bully me and make my life a living hell. Worst of all, I did not have enough of anything. I did not have enough space, food, books, privacy, dresses, shoes, toys, silence, or parenting. Soon, there would be one more sibling that I would be compelled to share with. That sibling, a boy, was followed by three more—a girl and two boys—so, when I was twelve years old, my immediate family consisted of two parents and eight children, all living in a row house with two roomers. It was too much to bear.

By the time I reached puberty, Chee Chee, a high-school student, was pregnant by her teen-aged boyfriend. In spite of merciless beatings, visits to and by the police, and constant shouted arguments, my parents had been unable to keep the two lovers from meeting secretly at the boy's home when his parents were at work and when they were both supposed to be in class.  My mother insisted that the newborn son be brought straight to our house  from the  hospital, and the two teenagers married shortly thereafter. The father joined the Air Force and my older sister exchanged physical and verbal child abuse for spousal abuse. Of course, she ended up pregnant a few months later with a baby girl. Unsuccessful suicide attempts and serious mental illness followed this grim scenario, which eventually became the plot for my oldest  brother's life story, too.

I was determined not to share my poor sister's fate so I knew I had to do the opposite of what she did. Most importantly, I would have nothing sexual or physical to do with boys, and I would neither openly rebel against nor actively seek to please my parents. Unlike my older and younger sister, when I graduated from high school, I had not engaged in any sexual activity. My burning ambition for years was to be a school teacher and, for that, I needed a college education. I also had to go to college so that I could learn more about the world that reading had shown me.

Upon graduation from high school, my first job was cashiering at a low-end family-owned department store. I was the second black female hired at the store, which also employed two black men as janitors. Everyone else was white. One of the janitors would become my lover in less than two years.

Our sexual relationship began casually for him, but explosively for me. When the store got extremely busy, Walter Lamb was required to abandon his cleaning duties and was pressed into service as a bagger. For several hours, we worked side-by-side behind a waist-high counter. Eventually, over a period of many months, he seduced me. Walt worked full time as an airplane mechanic in the Air Force. He was married, had a little boy, and he looked like a little bad boy himself. His hair was curly black, his skin was medium brown, and his eyes were light amber with dark flecks scattered in them. He had high, square cheekbones accentuated by deep dimples that flashed when he smiled crookedly. A perfectly square dimpled chin matched his broad shoulders and tiny waist. He switched a high, tight butt when he walked and he trod lightly, with slightly bowed legs. He had flirty glances and comments for all the ladies in his vicinity, and they all flirted back because he oozed sexuality with an effortless grace.

Also with effortless grace, Walt inserted his fingers into my crotch at every opportunity. His nimble fingers reduced me to breathless panic about twice a month as I made change from the cash register for customers who had no idea what was happening beneath my skirt. After a few months,

20

I could not take any more fondling from this sophisticated man, who was nearly thirty years old. I had to have him. When I told him that, he chuckled softly. "You're just a baby," he said. "I'm not a baby," I countered. "I'm a woman and I know what I want—and I want to have sex with you." He teased me. "You don't know anything," he said. "You're still a virgin." We argued some more and I told him that my virginity had nothing to do with it. He didn't agree. "I don't want to be responsible for your first sexual experience," he argued. "I don't do virgins. It's just too much pressure. I learned my lesson on that subject when I was much younger, and it had not turned out well. Just drop the subject," he demanded.

When I arrived at the store the next evening, I was an object of ridicule. The cashier whom I relieved and the dress department manager spoke for all my coworkers. "Is it really true that you are a virgin and that you asked that no-good Walter for sex?" So he thought he could shame me into giving up? Now this was a challenge! "Yes, so what?" I replied with a sophisticated toss of my head. They snickered even louder. I did not tell them about the sneaky fondling. It was none of their business.

The next day, I confronted Walt. "Would you have sex with me if I were not a virgin?" I asked him. He tried to hide his shock but, when he said yes, it sounded like he meant it. My next step was clear. I had to figure out whom to have sex with so that I could have sex with Walt. I had the perfect candidate—a boy who had been following me around for two years. I would soon execute the plan.

Corey's sloppy, wet kisses and fumbling hands were slightly repugnant. We had gone to the theatre and dinner together several times, and he had met me when I was crowned queen of Columbia Beach, where my family had a summer home on the Chesapeake Bay. He packed grease on his bone-straight hair to make it appear to be dark and curly. His very light skin and Bob Hope ski-jump nose made him look white at first glance, but his thick, wide lips betrayed his African American heritage.

His poor dental hygiene and saliva-drenched mouth made me hold my breath when he kissed me. Corey was accustomed to fondling me through my clothes for hours and then being firmly sent back home after a date. It took me a few weeks to find Corey again, re-establish the connection, and get him to agree to a tryst at the apartment he shared with his father. There, Corey removed every item of my clothing at the bedroom door, as if he were unwrapping a precious, fragile Christmas gift, and then he tenderly laid me on the bed. Although Corey was my age, he turned out to be an experienced lover who had been tutored in advanced sexual technique by a much older woman. He made sure that he did not cause me pain and that I had a series of quite wonderful orgasms before he did. In a few years, Corey would descend rapidly into a mental illness so profound that he was institutionalized off and on for decades. After a few sessions in the apartment, I figured that I was ready for Walt who had been ignoring me since our virginity argument.

One evening shortly thereafter, I cornered Walt for a private conversation. "I did it," I said proudly. He looked at me blankly. "You've done what?" He had no idea what I was talking about. "I had sexual intercourse. I'm not a virgin anymore. Now can we fuck?" My carnal experiences had made me even bolder since our last encounter. It never occurred to me that I just might be more trouble than I was worth. His mouth fell open in astonishment. I had rendered him speechless. "Do you want me to prove it?" A few weeks later, I *did* prove it to him, in the Bluebird Motel, somewhere in rural Maryland. When we entered the shabby room, he immediately headed for the tiny bathroom and shut the door. I stood beside the bed and waited patiently for him to emerge and undress me. He finally reappeared, naked from the waist down, and was surprised to see me standing there. "Why haven't you undressed and gotten under the sheet?" he asked. I had no short answer to that so I awkwardly took my clothes off for the first time in front of a man and climbed into the dingy bed. Walt joined me and ejaculated as soon as he touched my bare torso. Confused and embarrassed, I had no idea what had happened. "Have I done something wrong?" I asked. He just chuckled, and we finally accomplished what I hoped we both wanted to do.

We remained enthusiastic lovers for several years, although—after getting him drunk and "tricking him"—his wife had a baby boy during the relationship. Our affair ended when he told me that he was getting shipped out to Turkey. "Why are you leaving?" I asked. "To get away from you," he replied calmly. I really was more trouble than I was worth. Heartbroken, I got married while he was overseas. I showed him! The only sexually frustrating aspect of our encounters had been that he refused to allow me to fellate him, no matter how much I begged him. I had never done it before but I knew what I wanted. He was beautiful and fragrant, and just looking at his perfectly-shaped, rock-hard organ always made my mouth water. Explaining his refusal, he said, "If you do me, then you will expect me to do you and you will soon resent the fact that I will not do you, and we will argue about it." He would never reciprocate—could not—because he found the thought of putting his mouth anywhere near a vagina to be revolting. In fact, he never even looked at my crotch. Walt ignored my protestations and we had several wrestling matches related to the issue. He always won those.

Walt used jet-engine parts in stock cars for racing, which is illegal. In small towns all over the eastern shore of Maryland, I sat in rickety grandstands or stood among crowds along a road while he competed against other drivers who admired his mechanical work but had no idea that they were gazing at state-of-the-art jet airplane parts beneath the hood. Walt's fascination with fast cars was amazing to me because I had no interest in the cars or the sport.

With Walt, I attended house parties for the first time. At these events, I met and drank with all of his friends, who never mentioned his wife or children. His best friend was a convicted felon with five children and a grey-eyed, willowy, cheerful, exhausted wife. They were in love. The husband had established a pattern of obtaining employment in a variety of federal government jobs. Because the personnel offices took about a year to discover his felony conviction, he was gainfully employed for short periods of time over a number of years. It took me a while to figure out that, when we came to visit them, Walt gave his buddy enough money to allow them all to have dinner and see a movie while we enjoyed the privacy of their cluttered apartment. Soon, they stopped pretending that they were obliged to visit her mother when we showed up for a visit.

Silky, curly black hairs sprouted from Walt's upper lip, forming a thick, drooping moustache. They also sprouted from his upper chest down to his navel in a thick mat, and he always wore his shirt unbuttoned to reveal a strategic six inches of his nutmeg-colored chest. A magnetic attraction existed between him and all nearby women, to a shocking degree. In a crowded automobile en route to some alcohol-drenched party, Walt proceeded to tease several women about their breast size, accusing them of stuffing their bras with tissue paper. One of the women stripped to the waist and turned around to demonstrate to Walt that she did so have very large breasts and that her underwear was not padded. We all howled and doubled over in laughter. For Walt, this was a typical female reaction. I never saw him engage in any exercise other than vigorous sexual activity, which he eventually ended with a slight whisper of exhaustion followed by a near coma. His shoulders, abdomen, and arms were knotted with ropy muscles and his tiny waist, trim buttocks, and bow legs made him look quite feminine from the navel down. His body was covered with poreless, honey-smelling skin and I could never get enough of it. Our relationship became so intense that something terrible had to happen—and it did.

Walt and his wife had a terrible row one evening about his frequent absences from home. He became distraught and resentful, and confessed to her that he was in the midst of an affair with me that had already lasted many months. She had seen me at the department store and she knew who I was and what a baby I appeared to be. While his wife accused him of lying about the identity of his new lover, I accused him of putting my life in danger and, in less than a month, he got himself shipped out to Turkey. So much for confession being good for the soul. Luckily for me, my next significant sexual relationship was with my future husband, who had the same first name. When I called out a name in the throes of passion, it would be the right one.

*Me, about four years old.*

# Scene Seven
## High Yellow

When I was very young, I learned that I was ugly. I started kindergarten in the same public elementary school that my older siblings attended. My teacher, Mrs. Duckworth, was obsessed with the appearance of the children and, every morning, she inspected each of us. She was especially critical of the little boys, who were required to wear a white shirt and necktie to school daily; those who did not conform were sent home immediately. She shouted that the boys had to have their "kinky and beady hair combed" daily. During that year, I decided that something was wrong with my lips. They were too big. I began to lick and suck my upper lip compulsively and, soon, a dark scab formed over my entire upper lip area. My classmates quickly christened me "Three Lipsy, the Gypsy." They chanted the name at me in large groups whenever they saw me outside the classroom and, before long, the entire school adopted the name for me.

That year, my hair was very long and thick. I also had dark sideburns trailing down the lower edges of my face. In a few months, the scab had probably healed and the children tired of calling me "Three Lipsy, the Gypsy." They replaced it with "Elvis," after the popular singer, Elvis Presley. When I ran the five blocks home, I was serenaded by the new chant. Then, as I reached my house, a new hell awaited me. The block we lived on was changing from elderly white homeowners, who were moving to the suburbs, to young black families from the South, who were renters. My family was one of the few light-skinned nonwhite families on the block. Near my front yard, the chant became "Black is a race but yellow is a disgrace!"

Inside my house, the situation was even worse. My father called all of us collectively "animals" in Spanish, but I got special attention. Periodically, he gazed into my baby face and then turned aside mumbling in near wonderment, almost to himself, "You have a face just like a pumpkin." My mother's and older sister's thin, straight, silky hair had not prepared them for my thick, wavy, woolly, bushy mane and, on the rare occasions when it got combed at all, they took turns yanking and pulling my long hair out by the roots. It was styled in two braids that fell down my back like tangled ropes because they rarely got redone.

My clothes certainly did not make me look pretty. I grew very slowly, so Chee Chee and my mother were always several dress sizes larger than me. Thus, their hand-me-downs wore out before they ever fit me. My school uniforms, shoes, and Sunday dress were all purchased several sizes too big for me and, by the time I grew into them, the hems and edges were in tatters. Finally, my facial expression had to make me ugly. I had slowly added to my childhood survival list over the years and an important rule on that list was never to smile. Of course, it was not a difficult rule to follow. There was little in my childhood to smile about.

When I was transferred to Catholic school, the chants from schoolmates ended. In a couple of years, however, a gang evolved from the Catholic school girls who took a dislike to my hair. These students were new transfers from a nearby black Catholic school or from public schools, as integration had come to the private school system shortly after my arrival in the second grade. They pulled my hair and teased me about it on a regular basis. "Look at her hair," they said. "I'll bet it's not even real. Let's see if it's real. *You* pull it! No, you pull it, first. Oh, it's *so* ugly!" I rarely left the playground without one of my pigtails getting yanked. I was in my wanting-to-be-a nun and being-a-perfect-person phase, so I ignored my tormentors, turning the other cheek to them. That merely enraged them even more. Much too often, they chased me home from school and pushed me to the sidewalk. A passing postal worker probably saved my life or limbs one sunny afternoon when he scared off a group of about eight girls. The biggest one had already picked me up and flipped me over her right shoulder and onto the sidewalk  like a sack of potatoes.

Many years later, I was shopping in a jewelry store in St. Thomas, Virgin Islands,  trying to explain my rigid jewelry and clothing color preferences to a patient, ebony-colored sales clerk. "I hate the color of my skin," I whined to her, shoving the inside of my naked wrist at her.  "See that?" I demanded. "It's *yellow*—and it's *disgusting!*" I never wore yellow or pink tones because I was "high yellow," I explained in despair, using the derogatory term that my neighbors had used to describe me all my life. She asked me what the term meant and I repeated for her the chant with which I had grown up: "Black is a race and yellow is disgrace." She clicked her tongue softly and, in saintly sympathy, shook her head slowly. "In my country," she said, "your color is considered to be very beautiful. We call you mango-colored, like the flesh of the mango fruit. You are not yellow. *That* is yellow," she added, pointing to a bunch of bananas for sale on the sidewalk. "Thank you very much for saying that to me," I said, trying to hide the tears that had suddenly sprung to my eyes.

As a child, I performed a great variety of chores. One of my earliest memories is of using paint remover and a broad metal chisel to scrape paint off the woodwork in the living room. The odor turned my stomach and the old paint came away looking like rotten cottage cheese. Our old splintery wooden floors also had to be refinished periodically and I was in charge of spreading the glue-like shellac evenly over the surface with a broad brush that I wielded carefully as I crawled over the boards. Probably the most important chore I had  was scratching my mother's dandruff, and then rolling her long hair on strips of twisted paper bags, to make curls. But I was unable to perform hair-related tasks perfectly, so these were occasions for close-proximity verbal abuse, such as "What the hell is wrong with you? Are you so *stupid* you can't tell the damn paper is twisted wrong?" She swiftly followed these remarks with a hard slap across the face. As I grew older, I also became the coffee-maker for my mother, who consumed many cups a day.

I performed many tasks for my younger siblings, from baby-bottle sterilizer and formula maker to middle-of-the-night bottle feeder, diaper-changer, and baby comforter. In addition, my cleaning duties came to include hand washing and bleaching clothes and linens, hanging them to dry on the outdoor clotheslines, and ironing—especially starched blouses and shirts for school uniforms, though all of my father's clothes, including his socks, were cleaned and laundered professionally outside the home and his shirts were starched, folded, and kept in cardboard boxes that were stacked in the hall closet. By age ten, I had become the family cook.

After purchasing and carrying the groceries with a brother every day, I cooked dinner for eight to ten people, including my two parents. After dinner every night, I washed and dried the dishes with the assistance of various siblings.

I scrubbed the linoleum kitchen floor, made sure everybody had hot oatmeal each school morning, fixed baloney sandwiches for bag lunches, and got everyone dressed and out to school. In the morning, if we made too much noise, my mother emerged from her bedroom with a baby in tow and cursed us out of the house. "What do you think you're doing, leaving this house a damn mess like this?" she'd yell. "Pick that towel up from the floor and make sure you put the rest of that meat away or I'll get the belt right now." I was happy to escape from the house to the relative calm of the school building, and I hated summers.

My mother was a perpetually pregnant housewife. She used the pregnancies as an excuse to perform housework by proxy, bullying and threatening her children to execute a mind-numbing variety of tasks perfectly. It was not unusual for her to decide at midnight that the concrete basement floor needed painting, in which case she supervised as we washed the floor before we finished the paint job by dawn. A beautiful, curvaceous, vain woman, she blamed us for ruining her figure, which she displayed for us in a variety of waist-cinchers, girdles and lacy underwear. As soon as my father walked out the door in a fresh shirt to start his second job in the evening, she began the perfume, makeup, and hair rituals that transformed her for her evening trysts. All of us enthusiastically welcomed my mother's secret boyfriends and, as soon as they walked out the door, the games began.

The games consisted of terrorizing and pummeling each other with mops, plungers, brooms, and other weapons, which we fashioned from household objects. We chased each other through the house and over the roofs, locked each other up in the basement and in the bathrooms, and barely stopped short of maiming each other by the time Mama returned, pretending that she had never left for the evening. "I wonder why all the brooms have broken handles," she sometimes muttered to herself before she replaced them. We never told her that we had broken them over each other's heads during our nightly games.

Mama's weapon of choice (which we never used on each other) was a leather belt, but she also wielded clothesline rope, extension cords, and long, whip-like tree branches that had been stripped of their leaves by the trembling prospective victim. I discovered that it is just as horrific and traumatic to watch someone getting a terrible whipping as to receive one myself. As the recipient, concentrating too much on my own pain, I could not fully appreciate the expression of pure joy on Mama's face as she wielded her weapon. Likewise, I could not comprehend the sheer violence of the act that was so strenuous that Mama had to stop and rest to catch her breath—or was she having an orgasm? Too grateful for the brief respite, I never bothered to fathom the cause of it. "You stupid, no-good bastard," she screamed. "I should have *never* given birth to you! I told you time and time again not to leave the iron sitting on the board like that. Look what you did! You ruined my favorite gown! I'm going to kill you! Or maybe I should just throw you out of the house now. I'll call the police to come get you. Nobody else would raise you! Where do you think you would go, with your goddamn skinny legs and ugly face? *Damn* you!" Finally, the roaring in my ears would shut out the flow of invectives that accompanied each volley of blows.

I watched Chee Chee and Tony, my older siblings, receive whippings that drew blood, caused them to scurry across the floor like crabs on all four legs, and left them shivering and talking to themselves as they huddled in a corner to escape the blows. Mama most enjoyed the whippings when one of them cried the loudest, shed the most tears, and begged the most. "Mama, please stop," they would plead. "I won't do it again. I promise to be good. I *promise*, I promise!" But her enjoyment initiated a surge of seemingly bottomless energy as she meted out punishment for some imagined dereliction or disobedience. Eventually, she padlocked both the refrigerator and the pantry to prevent the most serious transgressions—the theft of food, including oranges, which were often left to rot. From witnessing these vicious, arbitrary whippings, I learned that it was best not to react to an act of violence that Mama initiated. The few times my mother whipped me, she quickly gave up out of boredom, confusion, or frustration as I stared her straight in the face, without flinching, turning my back, or begging her to cease. Under my breath, I recited my secret name for her—"You bitch, you bitch, you bitch, you bitch!"—as she tried to figure out what I was whispering, over and over. Indeed, she seemed to be puzzled by my reaction. I was seven years old and Chee Chee and Tony had taught me well, without intending to at all.

Daddy dispensed punishment in a different way. He was quick to anger, but the mood passed quickly too. Several times, I incurred his wrath for a trivial mistake, such as burning the rice that I prepared daily for his dinner. His specialty was a well-placed kick in the lower back, buttocks, or shin. Or he quickly reached out to grab me by the throat. I learned how to contend with his bursts of anger too. Even though my airflow was stopped immediately, and even though I knew that my neck would be sore and bruised for a week, I never moved to yank his hand away, never uttered a sound as he strangled me. I simply stared him coldly in the face. He always released me before I passed out and he soon tired of the violent act. Even after all these years, I cannot bear to wear a turtle neck sweater or any jewelry that touches the front of my throat.

My mother cursed us daily in English and my father did the same in his native language, Spanish. They both cursed each other. My mother loudly and constantly accused my father of having a sexual relationship with her older sister, who was a live-in nanny for her first child when my mother worked in the federal government. She discovered the two lovers together in the marital bed when she came home early with morning sickness during her second pregnancy. She threw the sister out, quit her job, and never worked outside the home again. My father had been secretly monitoring my mother's telephone conversations for years and he incessantly accused her of being a whore. When she obtained an illegal abortion after the birth of her seventh child, he followed her to the abortionist and confronted her. She gave birth to her last child, a towhead with Down's Syndrome, a year later. Upon her discovery of the telephone tap (ingeniously rigged from his darkroom in the basement), she ordered my brothers to destroy the entire room and its contents. They gleefully smashed walls, cameras, and equipment. My evening prayers from age six always began with a plea for a divorce, but that childhood request was not granted until I had moved out of the house.

My father was amazed and offended by the physiological fact that we required eight or more hours of sleep each night, when he required only six. Our normal nutritional needs were also a source of angst for him. Why did we have to eat so much and so often? We should have been able to subsist on one meal a day, like he did. "You are all lazy, and stupid, and no good," he said. "And you waste food and clothes too much." He stared at us as if we could argue with him. We were not supposed to grow out of shoes or coats. On these fundamental matters, my parents both agreed but they argued loudly and heatedly about everything else, especially money and the possibility of adultery. Nearly daily, they elicited bloodcurdling screams from Chee Chee and Tony. In the summer, the windows were usually open, and we lived in a row house. It always amazed me that nobody ever sent the police to our home when spring arrived.

In fact, one of the worst beatings Chee Chee ever got was administered in the front vestibule, at the top of the porch area, on an Easter Sunday. "I'm not going to wear that ugly straw hat to church," she shouted to Mama. "And you can't make me!" I knew what was coming next and none of us was surprised when Mama gave the order to get a switch. "Put the goddamn hat on your skinny head and take your yellow ass on to church!" Mama screamed as she began the session. "No, Mama, please don't make me do it," Chee Chee pleaded. "I hate that hat and I hate *you*. Why are you so mean to me? What have I ever done to *you*?" The big, blood-red straw hat was a hand-me-down and it made my pale sister look like a clown. But, soon, she was reduced to a fetal position in the corner of the small space, unable to escape the blows in the confined area. There was not even a chair to shield her. Her howls and moans circled the block and returned. Mama was out of control. "What have you *done*? You were *born*, you nasty little bitch! You're smelling yourself. You think you're so cute, but you're not. I should have never had you! I should have flushed you down the toilet. You're no good and I hate you, too. Don't you dare speak to me like that." Finally, exhausted, Mama got what she wanted from my mentally shattered sister. "I'm sorry, Mama. Please stop beating me. I'm sorry, I'm sorry! I'll never do it again. I'll wear the hat. Please stop…" I was nine years old, and nobody ever came to help us.

My childhood was  populated by a series of roomers.  While we shared bedrooms and bathrooms in the cramped row house, Mama advertised in local newspapers for weekly renters. If a woman showed up, she was told that the room was already rented. "They stink," Mama proclaimed. "They want to have visitors, they bleed all over everything, and they hang their wet underwear in the bathroom." So, she accepted only male renters, who paid cash every week. Like despised ghouls, they crept into and out of the attic and the basement at all hours of the day and night. They were not allowed to cook, wash clothes, or have visitors. A succession of drug addicts, drunks, and mentally unstable men passed through the family home until my mother's death at age eighty-six.

# Scene Eight
## Don't Hurt Me

It was not fair. Why did I have to suffer so much? Why was my life so difficult? I was thirteen years old and I had no friends, no toys, no pretty clothes, and no time to play or do my homework. It was past midnight. I had to go to school in the morning and, still, I patted my baby brother on his back as I walked with him across the floor to keep him from crying. But it had been a wonderful day. The day had been wonderful because my cousin Yvonne had come to visit. I had not seen her in several years and she looked older than me, although we were the same age. She certainly was taller than I was, by at least three inches, but I was the second shortest girl in my class. One blue-eyed blonde with huge ringlets down to her waist was always the shortest girl, and she was two inches shorter than me. She was *really* short. I was just short. Yvonne was just right. Her skin was exactly the same color as mine and her hair was the same length and texture as mine, too. How wonderful it was to spend time with a girl who looked like me.

Yvonne looked like me, but her life was nothing like mine. She brought dolls and a box full of games with her. We had spent the entire Sunday afternoon playing jacks, taking turns bouncing the tiny red ball and scooping up the metal spikes from the tiled vestibule floor. Then we played Old Maid, a card game that made Yvonne squeal with joy.

It was my job to watch my baby brother Mike, and to change his diaper, feed him, and keep him entertained. It was not easy for a thirteen-year-old, and his demands quite often interrupted my play time with Yvonne. Most of the time, I did not mind taking care of Mike. His skin was as smooth as rose petals and the color of the coffee in the percolator when I made coffee for Mama. His flesh was plump and firm, like peaches, and his head was covered with tight curls that my mother cut very short. His wide, slanted eyes and brown smiling mouth showed the world that

Mike was a happy baby—happy and smart. Although he was not even six months old, I was able to teach him how to count the stars up to fifty, and he could name all the parts of his body when I pointed to them. Just that week, he had begun to speak in short phrases and he was crawling and, in another month, he would probably be walking. While I played with Yvonne, Mike wanted to play with the cards, and he almost tore them. Yvonne was angry with him.

She was an only child, with pretty clothes, shiny patent leather shoes, and hair fixed at the beauty parlor. Why couldn't I be an only child? Why is my house filled with noise and confusion? It would be different if I had no brothers or sisters. Maybe then my mother and father would have conversations with me and I could ask them questions. When I made a mistake and tried to explain what I thought was the right way to wash the floor or fry the chicken, Mama would not say, "Then you thought like Lit. Lit thought he fart but he shit!" I was proud of Mike and wanted Yvonne to like him, so I tried to explain to her that Mike was a good baby and that he was just trying to play with us.

"Why don't you put him to sleep?" asked Yvonne. The answer was obvious. If Mike slept during the day, he would stay awake all night. Although my mother was a housewife, it was *my* responsibility to care for Mike during the night. If he woke during the night, I had to heat the bottle for him and sit with him in the kitchen until he fell back to sleep. Only then could I creep upstairs with him and knock softly on my parents' door to return him to the crib in the corner. There was no point explaining this to Yvonne. The interruptions were making her angry and she did not care what happened after she left. If I did not put the baby to sleep, she might stop playing with me.

Because Mike was a good baby, all I had to do was give him a warm bottle, rock him gently, and tell him to go to sleep several times in a soft voice. In less than fifteen minutes, I was able to put Mike down for a four-hour nap. Yvonne and I resumed playing our games while everyone else went to the back yard to admire my mother's roses. She had a green thumb and her boyfriends drove her to nurseries all over the suburbs to buy unique varieties for her garden. They all had long thorns and the blooms were so huge that they filled the alley behind our house with their sickening sweet perfume.

The house was quiet. Yvonne walked over to me and put her hand on my shoulder. "Let me show you something," she whispered. She stepped up to me and, for several minutes, kissed me on the mouth. Her tongue probed my teeth, the roof of my mouth, and the soft tissue under my tongue. I wanted to be a nun, and I knew temptation when it presented itself. As a devout Catholic, I spent every day in a quest for perfection, determined to avoid sin in thought, word, and deed. I broke off the kiss and we resumed our card game.

Rubbing the baby's back, I thought about the kiss. It was not fair. A wave of self pity washed over me. My parents should not be so mean. My mother should not have had any children and I should never have been born. I did not ask to be born. Why am I here? Why did I stop kissing Yvonne? Did somebody teach her how to kiss like that? Did she kiss boys too? How would it feel to kiss a boy? Would it be different? If I had put the baby to sleep earlier, maybe she would have kissed me sooner. If I did not have to take care of the baby, I might still be kissing her. Just then, the baby whimpered. I looked down at his shiny hair and I felt cheated—cheated of my childhood and cheated of happiness. In the midst of my misery, I pinched the baby's fat thigh, hard.

I got no response from him, but I needed someone to be as miserable as I was and I knew he was still awake. I pinched his thigh again, even harder this time. Instead of the baby's sobs and tears, I felt and heard a small sigh escape from Mike's rounded chest. "Please don't hurt me again," he said loud and clear. It was his first sentence. He was innocent and I had been mean to him. He had not asked to be born, either, and I had committed a terrible sin, sin that grew out of self pity—an emotion that I had struggled with for years. I had also done wrong out of anger, and anger had terrible consequences. I had seen what my parents' anger had done to my older siblings already, as they were cruelly beaten. We were all  cursed, derided, and threatened with being thrown out of the house and sent to Junior Village, the foster home. Because I was still religious, I bowed my head and touched Mike's soft, tight curls with my chin. I knew how to pray and I believed in God. "God, please help me so that I will not be a mean person like my mother," I prayed. "The baby is innocent. Please help me not to take anything out on him again, no matter how bad it gets. Let me recognize self-pity and overcome it. Please keep me from destroying myself and others with anger.  I am frightened, and tired and weak. Please help me to be brave and strong, and to be a good person. Amen." I apologized to Mike and then I walked him until he fell asleep.

An example of my parents' behavior illustrates well the complex relationship between them. It was summertime, shortly after my graduation from high school, and my mother's new secret lover had convinced her to buy a beach house across the street from his, at Columbia Beach, a black private beach on the Chesapeake Bay. While I worked full time in the city, Mama and my siblings were ensconced in the beach house for their fourth summer. My father worked at his federal government job in the daytime and at his other two jobs in the evenings, so he only sometimes joined the family at the beach house on weekends. I paid rent to my mother as if I were a roomer. Like them, I had no visitors and did no cooking, though I did wash my clothes in the basement.

I never asked my father to give me a ride to work in the morning. He just started doing it my second week on the job. "I will drive you to work," he said simply. It was a great relief for me and I thanked him profusely when he did, because the alternative was a bus ride and transfers that took over an hour and that made me sick to my stomach. I was cursed with motion sickness. The car ride added less than ten minutes onto his usual commute to the Library of Congress, which was halfway to my job. But, after several weeks, he spoke to me one morning. "I will not drive you to work any longer," he informed me. Although I was not in the habit of questioning or arguing with either of my parents, I asked without thinking, "Why not?" I was really hurt. "Your mother told me I cannot do this anymore," he announced, turning away from me. He obviously had told her that he was driving me to work. I was astounded at this turn of events, first that he had told her and, secondly, that she would be mean enough to deprive me of a kindness that cost her nothing. Irrational and unfair, the act was consistent with her controlling personality structure. "There is no way she could possibly know whether you are still driving me to work," I said to Daddy. "So why don't you just ignore what she told you to do?" He just shook his head and walked out of the room. The subject was closed. Every time I caught the bus that sweltering summer, I marveled at the power that Mama exerted over the entire family. My passive, angry father watched his children get whipped worse than dogs, and he found it impossible to continue to perform even one charitable act for me against her wishes. I was so upset that, the next day, I went to a fancy department store and shoplifted a pink fuzzy sweater, which I never wore.

*My father at work.*

# Scene Nine

Passing

Clarence said often that I was the only person he knew who had chosen their own race. My father's roots are in Spain, in a small town where his large, extended family owned dairy farmland and probably some small businesses. At some point in the nineteenth century, one or both of his parents emigrated to the Philippine Islands, where his family owned a match factory and a general store. My father was born there, and one of his parents was probably born there too. Certainly, neither one of my paternal grandparents was black. As a young man, my father emigrated to Cuba, where he married and sired a daughter. Shortly after the natural death of his young wife, he made his way from Cuba to the United States, without the child. When my parents met, my father was a federal government employee with a strong work ethic, a thick Spanish accent, and a youthful appearance. Slender and dapper, he wore a suit and tie to work every day and owned a large collection of hats and smoking pipes. His wavy hair and moustache were always neatly dyed and trimmed. Calligraphy and photography were the means by which he earned a living but, at some point, he had also been a ship's cook and a manual laborer. At the Library of Congress, he operated a photo-duplicating machine that copied books and, at night, he photographed patrons and performers at the Lotus nightclub, a fancy supper club downtown. There he had a camera girl and a darkroom, and he shared profits with the club owners. Although his formal education probably ended in his teen years, he was an avid newspaper reader and political junkie.

My maternal grandmother was probably half Cherokee and half white, a tobacco-chewing, stocky diabetic who looked like a nineteenth-century squaw when she came to live with us for several months. The family story was that, when the children went to my great-grandmother's house, they had to enter through the kitchen because my grandmother had been disowned when she married her colored sweetheart. My maternal grandfather was African American, dark skinned and slender in his photographs. As a young child, he was taken in and adopted by a white family, who raised him apart from his birth siblings. I never met him. He loved the city, where he ran a lucrative business, but his wife refused to leave the farm, and so they were divorced by the time my mother left for Washington, D.C. to join her aunt and young cousins.

A few months after their meeting in a park, my parents eloped. My mother got a job as a typist in the federal government, where she worked until the birth of her second child. My mother matured to become a long-haired, curvy brunette with Asian features. Her skin was light and prone to freckles and sunburn. The first child born of the marriage was my sister, nicknamed Chee Chee. Lighter than either of her parents, she had straight hair, which was also much lighter than theirs. Chee Chee always looked white. As she aged and gained weight, she began to look just like my mother's youngest sister, Buttercup. Singled out for the most verbal and physical abuse, however, Chee Chee has spent most of her adult life in psychiatric care.

The second child, a boy nicknamed Tony, had straight black hair and was slightly darker than my father. He later grew to look like an East Indian, just like my father's youngest brother, Anthony, who came to visit us. Tony was very close in age and temperament to Chee Chee and, like her, he was subjected to emotional and physical abuse. He also spent most of his adult life in mental institutions. My mother gave birth to six additional children, all different shades with totally different hair textures. In birth order, I was a middle child, fourth from the oldest and fifth from the youngest. I also had middle family skin color and middle family hair texture.

When we started school, we all went to the neighborhood black schools. We lived in a black neighborhood and the roomers, relatives, and adults we associated with in our home were mostly black. Racial labeling was a source of great interest in my home. When my darkest brother, Mike, was brought home from the hospital as a newborn, Mama laid him on the dining room table so that all of us could crowd around and touch him. Daddy stood nearby, gazing intently at the tiny dark red, round face and thick, bluish hair. "He looks just like a monkey," he said before he walked into the hall.

Although we never discussed exactly why we did it, all of us spent hours comparing skin and lip color to determine who had the darkest skin. Two of my brothers (one older and one younger than me) went to work at the nightclub with my father when they were about twelve years old. Since they were the two lightest boys, I assumed they passed for white in the segregated restaurant. I assumed the same in reference to my three siblings who usually accompanied my mother to Glenn Echo Amusement Park, Garfinckel's Department Store, and other segregated venues. I was never chosen for such forays into the all-white world and, as a result, I thought of myself as completely black. I never even considered attempting to pass or being mistaken for white.

After taking a trip to Georgia, Clarence and I had a long conversation about my racial identity. "How could you possibly think I look white?" I demanded. Amazed to learn for the first time that Clarence thought I looked white, I was even more shocked when he said, "All my family members, including my mother, think you are white." Suspecting that he was making a joke and kidding me, I challenged him. "Prove it," I said. I was getting upset but he was having a good time. He threw his head back and laughed with his mouth wide open, revealing every tooth in his head. "Okay, you'll see," he said. "That will be really easy!" We were in his new apartment in Maryland. Without getting up, he called out to his son, Jamal. "Come here a minute, Son," he said. "I have a question to ask you. It won't take long and then you can get back to your homework." Jamal, ten years old, was curious when he ran into the living room, where we were seated. "What is it, Dad? I'm almost finished with my homework, anyway." Clarence pointed at me, still smiling. "What race is she?" Jamal looked confused and asked, "What do you mean?" Clarence smiled. "Is Lillian black or white?" he asked, more specifically. Jamal looked at his father as if he were insane. "She's white, Dad," he replied. Then he sighed heavily and rolled his eyes. Sometimes Dad could be so silly! Jamal walked into his bedroom to finish his homework.

# Scene Ten

### The Creep

Maybe I should have known that Peter was a rapist. I was only nineteen years old, but I knew he was a creep, even though he was a tall, muscular, handsome guy. He had been following me around for several months, catching the bus with me and telling me in an intense whispery voice how beautiful I was. We were both college students with part-time jobs, so I had no reason to socialize with him. Besides, he appeared to be in his thirties, and I was already in a complicated relationship with an older man.

In spite of the fact that my sexual experiences involved only a handful of men, I thought I had them figured out. They were amusing and fun and they could provide me with orgasms, which I have never been good at producing on my own. I also thought that my years of battling with my brothers had toughened me so that I had nothing to fear from men, since I had won most of the fights. I was wrong.

One evening, I was tired and hungry when Peter jumped onto the bus with me. The little old church ladies around us smiled as he went into his usual monologue, begging me to have dinner with him and two other couples. At that point, I made the mistake that I imagine many women have made when a persistent man has gotten on that last nerve and worn them down. I agreed to go out with him so that I could get rid of him.

On the night of the dinner date, I decided that I would have some fun with Peter, since I would not be going out with him again. I chuckled as I slipped into my sexiest garter belt, fishnet stockings, and lace panties. Some teasing would be on the menu. I knew that the site for the dinner was a large home that had been converted illegally into a private club. I had been there for some fraternity parties and I'd enjoyed myself there. I could not dance, but I always enjoyed listening to the deafening music and watching others twirl and gyrate on the dance floor as I ate and sipped drinks with my date. That night, when Peter picked me up, we joined a car packed with couples who were headed to the same venue. The couples soon separated and I ended up in a booth with Peter. I had never been intoxicated and I could not tell whether the gin was making me groggy or whether Peter had slipped a pill into the second mixed drink he pressured me to consume. In a couple of hours, Peter had his fingers firmly wedged into my crotch and I was on my tenth orgasm, all hidden from view by the darkness and a long tablecloth.

When Peter murmured that we would go to a more private area, I was too dazed to reply. I simply allowed him to extricate me from the booth. Leaving the music and dancers behind, I stumbled up the narrow, dark stairs and I knew that I was in trouble. Peter pushed a door open. I spied a narrow bed in a cramped room. I would be alone with the creep. "What the fuck do you think you're doing, you son of a bitch?" I protested loudly, shoving him in the chest in order to get back into the hall. Peter said nothing. With one arm, he easily pushed me onto the bed and, with the other, he closed the door and locked it. I struggled to move my sluggish body from the mattress as Peter groped at my underwear. I flung myself from the bed and went for the door. This time, Peter got me by the throat. He fell on top of me and gripped my garter belt at the waist. With a surge of adrenaline, I twisted away from him and cursed him loudly again. "Get the fuck off me!" I screamed. "Go to hell and leave me alone, you goddamn creep!"

By then, my eyes had adjusted to the darkened room. Peter pushed himself up onto his elbows and held his face immobile just six inches from mine as he pinned me to the bed with his legs and torso. "Listen to me, Lillian," he said calmly, in a voice that I later heard emanating from my sociopath male clients, who had been charged with violent offenses. "If you do not take your underwear off yourself, I will punch you so hard that I will break your nose and your face, and nobody in this house will come to help you when you scream." Looking at him, I saw something I recognized. It took me a second to figure out how, but it was the same expression my mother wore when she was in the midst of exhausting herself while whipping Chee Chee with a belt, an extension cord, or a switch from the backyard tree. It was joy, lust, and power. It was pure evil. His transformation from a creepy, normal guy to a serial rapist was complete.

I turned my face toward the wall as I pulled the panties down, so that I would not have to look at him. He huffed and puffed his way to ejaculation during the two-minute rape. Afterwards, I said nothing to him or to anyone else in the house or in the car. I got dressed, went down the stairs, and rode home in the same vehicle that had transported me earlier.

The next day, the telephone calls began. "I want to make up for what happened. Please see me again. It was all your fault, you know." Each time, when I recognized his voice, I hung up in a panic. Then, he started appearing at my job. It occurred to me that he might start out every relationship with a rape and that mine was probably not the first one—and would not be the last. Everybody knew that "date rapes" were not prosecuted in Washington, D.C. then, especially when the victim did not end up in the emergency room for stitches or a cast.

One evening, Peter happened to come by the store when Walt was there. I had told Walt about the rape and the telephone calls. "That's the guy," I whispered to Walt as I pointed out Peter, who had taken up his usual post against a wall. He was watching me out of the corner of his eyes, trying to blend in with the customers in the shoe department. Walt stared at Peter. "I know, Lillian," he said. "How could you *possibly* know?" I asked. "I saw you change when he walked onto the floor," Walt said. "You're still afraid of him." Walt was right. My hands were trembling. I stared at him and nodded. "Don't worry," Walt said with a crooked smile. "I'll take care of it for you." He sauntered off the floor and, a few minutes later, Peter

crept down the same stairs. Walt and I never spoke again about the matter, and I never heard from or saw Peter again.

# *Scene Eleven*

## On the Stage

I was born to act, being gifted with the ability to slip easily into another world and to hide what I might be thinking. I was also comfortable speaking to an audience. My experience as an actor began in the first grade and ended in college, on the day Martin Luther King was assassinated. In the first grade, I was selected to be traffic safety queen, for some reason that was never revealed to me. I was told to memorize a rather lengthy speech, having something to do with the many ways children were killed in vehicular accidents in the crowded streets of Washington, D.C. After days of memorizing the lines in front of a cracked mirror at home, I was ready for the safety assembly rehearsal. As I recited the long speech flawlessly from memory, the sheer joy on the face of the teacher who had chosen me for the role was unforgettable. I was hooked. The next day, when I delivered the speech before the entire elementary school, the audience burst into spontaneous applause, and I was persuaded to give the speech a second time. By then, I was really hooked.

The next year, for reasons that were never satisfactorily explained to me, my parents transferred me and some of my siblings from public school to the nearby Catholic school, Saint Martin's. For several years, we were the only nonwhites. The nuns taught fifty-three students to a class, and my acting career was in hiatus for several years. With my entire class, I memorized daily catechism lessons, sang or chanted classical liturgical hymns, and presented oral book reports, but these were poor substitutes for my former performances. By the time I graduated from Saint Martin's School in the eighth grade, I had lost my faith.

When I started ninth grade, I entered public school and pretty much abandoned my earlier hopes of going to college. Although they never admitted it, neither of my parents had graduated from high school and, in many ways, it was made clear to me that the most I could aspire to was a secretarial position in the federal government, where I would work for some white executive type.

By the ninth grade, my childhood survival tactics had become fairly complex. For years, I neither rebelled against my parents nor sought actively to please them. I had discovered that my older siblings' rebellion was met with swift and cruel punishment. I also knew that it was impossible to please them, so my survival list included doing whatever I was told to do, volunteering for nothing, and asking for nothing. Thus, when the administration at the public junior high school asked me whether I would be in the business track or the college track, I chose business. That way, I reasoned, I could start working as soon as I graduated from high school and I would be able to pay my own tuition for college later. But, when they got my transcript a few weeks later, they realized the error. They tried to persuade me to switch to college preparatory, but it was too late. I had discovered that I could spend an entire year repeating the fourth grade curriculum from Catholic school. With the exception of typing, which I could never master, I was getting straight A's. As a result of the fluke, I ended up being valedictorian of my ninth-grade graduating class. My inability to type, however, ruined my plan of getting a secretarial job upon graduating from high school and my life plan was a wreck.

The teacher-organizer of the school's graduation ceremonies handed me a lengthy graduation speech that she had written several years earlier. She loved the speech but, due to its complexity and length, none of my predecessor speakers had been able to deliver it. At the graduation rehearsal a few days later, I delivered the speech from memory and she was astounded. At graduation, the applause for my speech nearly deafened me, and I loved it.

In high school, I narrated the Christmas plays. By senior year, I was allowed to join the Drama Club and I landed the female lead in *The*

*Boy Next Door*, a play about coming of age. The play included a love triangle and a senior-prom plot, and I pretended that I owned a prom dress for the part, though I never went to a prom because I refused to ask my parents for a prom dress, money, or any other clothing. If they did not notice that I had holes in my shoes, I just wore shoes with holes in them. The director ended up renting a dress and shawl for me. When I made my entrance onto the stage, someone in the wings yanked the shawl from my shoulders to reveal the strapless gown that I wore beneath it. I did not discover until the end of scene one that the entire time I had been perched on top of a three-foot-high wall, my dress had been hitched up to my waist on the left side of my garter belt.

Through most of the play, two boys argued over me until, finally, I had a kissing scene with the victor. In rehearsal, my costar and I always joked about the scene, so that, when the real event had to occur on stage, we were completely unprepared for it. The teacher-director had instructed me to put my arms around his shoulders, but the kiss itself was a total blank for me, and I had no idea what we were doing with our lips. The next day, a more sophisticated twelfth-grader asked, " What happened with that long kiss, girl?" I had no idea what she meant, and my facial expression must have made her realize that she had to be more specific. "Did you French or *what*?" she demanded. Time had stopped for me during the kiss—and I had no idea what Frenching was—so I said, "Yes, sure." She chuckled and smirked as if she had won a bet before she pranced away. For my role in the play, one of my classmates had applied my makeup. I was so impressed with the transformation that I did not wash my face for a month. I have been wearing makeup every day of my life since then, although I now wash my face more often. Before appearing in that play, I had not even worn lipstick, but mascara, eye shadow, eyeliner, rouge, foundation, lip liner, lipstick, and face powder had turned me into a woman in one hour.

My next theatrical venture would introduce me to my first white lover. In college, again I was cast as the love interest in a romantic comedy, *Two's Company*. Again, two males competed for my affections. One of the males was a tall, handsome, dark-haired, blue-eyed white student, who had done work in summer stock theater in New York State. After spending many hours in rehearsal with the cast, I arranged a sexual interlude with the gorgeous man. Although the act itself was satisfactorily completed, I was surprised to find him emotionally distant, silent, and strangely detached during the entire encounter.

On the night of the play's performance, everyone was nervous because the play required several costume changes and, in the last scene, I would wear a wedding dress. It turned out that my own wedding dress was perfect for the scene, but the two Drama Club members who would help me with my three costume changes would have to work very quickly to make sure that I did not miss my cues. For the first change, everything went smoothly but, for the second change, only one fellow student was backstage to help me with the zippers and buttons. I saw the other one standing in the wings, sobbing. "Oh, no," she cried over and over. "Oh, no!" The play was a comedy and she was not supposed to be crying. I was furious. For the final change, I was all alone backstage and had to dress myself quickly. When I emerged onto the stage, I noticed half the audience had left the theatre. Something was terribly wrong. Was the play really that bad? By the final curtain, the audience was politely applauding while they quietly filed out. When I finally left the sad theatre with my husband, his aunt whispered to me. "We just heard the news that the Reverend Martin Luther King was assassinated by a white man," she said. "Black neighborhoods are rioting and setting buildings on fire all over the country and all over the District, too."

Several weeks later, I ran into my white sex partner in the college library. "Did you like the sex we had together?" I asked. I really was curious about his odd behavior. "I enjoyed something quite different much more than what we did together," he replied calmly. Then he walked away from me. I never had sex with him again, never found out what the more enjoyable experience might have been, and I never auditioned for another role. My acting career ended the day that Martin Luther King was shot.

### I Said, "Freeze!"

A white woman saved my life. It was Halloween week and I was a cashier in a department store. Before the doors opened to the public, we had to obtain "the bank" of fifty dollars in small bills and rolls of coins from the store manager so that we could make change and prepare for business. As we gathered on the first floor, Simon Fletcher, the manager, ran upstairs to the walk-in safe on the third floor to retrieve the cash. Simon had the large head, pug nose, stubby fingers and short extremities of a dwarf, but he was of average height. With a receding hairline, he appeared older than his thirty-six years, and he massaged the top of his head with both hands and yanked his hair when he got nervous, which was often. A few seconds after he went upstairs, we watched him creep back down the stairs with his fingers pressed to his thick lips for silence. He tugged on the hair on top of his head as if to rip it out by the roots, and motioned for us to follow him up the stairs. Like sheep, we all started shuffling silently toward his outstretched arms.

A silver-haired, glamorous, white woman stood to my left and three feet behind me. Hump-backed, skinny, and middle-aged, Terri Sand had always been nicer to me than my own mother. Though her nose had grown in her middle age, nearly meeting her upper lip when she smoked, Terri was wise and I followed her advice in all significant matters. For example, on my first day, when I reported for work as a cashier, my hair fell well below my shoulder blades and I wore it in one long, thick plait down the middle of my back. Terri harassed me about the hair for months. "That braid makes you look like a refugee just off the boat from China, darling," she said softly. As she frowned, a stained cigarette from her two-pack-a-day habit dangled from the edge of her lower crimson lip. She ate two fried egg sandwiches, one for breakfast and one for lunch, washed down with one of several cups of steaming black coffee. I did not want to cut my hair and waste time and money doing anything more complex than putting it into a plait every day. Indeed, it was so wavy and thick that hairdressers refused even to wash it. When I was in junior high school I had gotten it cut short at my mother's insistence and my hair emerged as a huge mass of bushy curls. I was shocked. "What happened to my wavy hair?" I asked the hairdresser. She sneered and laughed at me. "It was only the weight of your long hair that made it wavy. Everybody's hair gets curly and nappy when it's cut short," she explained, incorrectly.

I told none of this to Terri. I assumed that she did not care *why* my hair was too long. "It just is, darling." After a few months, I dutifully got my hair trimmed and then I went to a beauty salon every month to maintain the trendy style that Terri approved of. I also obeyed her in matters of attire. After all, she was the manager of the dress and coat department. Although I never bought my dresses from her department because they were too big for me, Terri determined whether I wore an outfit more than once after I had purchased it. "That looks lovely on you, dear," meant that the outfit would become my new favorite. A tough old broad, she ran the department with an iron fist. If a dress was too large for the customer and Terri knew that no smaller size was in stock, she gathered a handful of material in the back of the dress, twirled the customer to face the mirror, and said, "How *gorgeous* you look with a little tuck!" If the dress or coat was too small, she unbuttoned the outfit and said, "How lovely you look by simply moving the buttons over a little, here."

I had seen Terri cry only once. Facing the stairwell and the shoe department, I was working the cash register in the middle of the second floor, between domestics and the ladies' dress department. Simon came running down the stairs from the third-floor offices, flushed and breathless, tugging frantically at his hair. He pointed wordlessly at the public address system, a brown tweed speaker box mounted on the far wall next to the stairwell. He had turned the radio on before running down from the office.

The familiar voice of Walter Cronkite was booming over the selling floor. We stopped what we were doing to listen to the static-filled announcement. The voice was breaking, choking with unshed tears. "Repeating this bulletin," he said, "President Kennedy shot while driving in an open car from the airport in Dallas, Texas, to downtown Dallas…"

Customers and employees stood motionless, paralyzed. We stared at the tweed box. Finally, great sobs from Terri broke the silence. "I loved that man," she cried. "I love his family. Oh, no! Oh, no." Tears fell unchecked down her chin and dropped onto her bony chest. She reached across the counter and grabbed both of my hands for comfort. Her mascara ran and her face powder had tracks in it. Would her pencil-thin eyebrows disappear and her spray-painted silver bouffant hair now collapse? I was more shocked by Terri's reaction than I was by the assassination of my president.

A really great lady, Terri had always been nice to me. During that Halloween week, I looked to her for guidance as I slowly followed the other employees toward the stairwell, where the manager was still beckoning. On this day, as usual, Terri was dressed in a tight black sheath, pumps, and sheer stockings. Her bulging blue eyes and deep-set lids were accentuated by dark blue eye shadow and black mascara. Her eyebrows were painted silver to match her hair and, as usual, every strand of silver hair had been sprayed carefully in place. She had created rosebud lips by careful application of a brush and her face and neck wore matching pink from her face-powder compact. She appeared to be calm. Suddenly, two figures lunged from the alcove just behind Simon. They both wore elaborate, full-face gorilla masks and the taller one walked toward us with a large .45 caliber revolver in his hand. Both men had spent the night locked in the store, hiding in the basement, and then, in the morning, they had crept up to the second floor, where they donned the grotesque rubber masks, armed themselves, and confronted the manager on his way to the back offices.

I did not hear myself scream and I did not feel my legs running, but I was at the store's front door and about to yank it open when I heard Terri shouting loudly at me. Her voice penetrated the roaring in my head. "Lillian!" she screamed. "Stop!" With my hand still on the door, I whirled my head around. Terri stood with her arms around me, bravely facing down the gunman. Then I realized that he had rushed toward me and that he was ordering me to stop running. "Bitch," he shouted, "I said freeze! I said freeze!" He continued to curse me as he advanced, pointing the pistol at my head. "Get the *fuck* away from the door!" Terri had prevented me from attempting to open the front door, which was probably still locked. She had also prevented my getting shot in the back, and she had done it by placing her body between me and the weapon. In a flash, I knew what I had to do. I calmly raised my arms to the sky, walked forward—toward the pistol—and spoke to the masked figure. "I will go upstairs," I said. "I will go upstairs."

Upstairs, a few minutes later, we all watched as Simon knelt in front of the safe. His entire body shook as he fumbled to open the combination lock. Soon, like zombies, we followed the manager into the walk-in vault and allowed the robbers to close the door on us. They made their escape before the police were called. Terri had saved my life by nearly sacrificing her own. A few months later, I recalled that act vividly.

I was working the register with Cora, a prim, red-headed fiftyish spinster who had just been hired away from a local jewelry store. Talking about her experience there, Cora became agitated and angry as she described several robberies. Cora had been robbed at gunpoint at her register so many times that she had made a firm decision. "I will *never* be a victim again," she said, shaking her head and slamming her palm on the counter. "I'm sick of it!" Hoping that it would not happen to her again, she had switched from the jewelry store to the department store. Simon, the manager, had assured all of us that it would not happen again. "God forbid, if it does," he said, "just hand the money over. Don't be a hero! Just remember, it's not your money." Cora was not mollified. "It's not *about* the money," she told me. "It's about being helpless. I *hate* them!"

Following the Halloween robbery, management installed a panic button system at each cash register. The button was connected to an alarm in the manager's office. "When I hear the alarm," Simon promised, running his hands through his hair, "I will call the police!" We had a training session to make sure that we all knew how to use the system and to demonstrate that potential robbers would not be able to hear it. The problem with the system was that, one day, we were doing paperwork and pressed the button by mistake. The manager came barreling down the stairs. "What's the problem?" he yelled at the top of his lungs. "Is everything okay down here?" Although we both apologized for pressing the button and triggering a false alarm, we looked at each other and realized that the buzzer system was useless. It would just get all of us killed.

A couple of weeks later, Cora and I were working in the basement together. She was at the register while I was in the back room. Behind the counter, a narrow corridor led to boxes of merchandise in the layaway department. If a customer wanted merchandise that they could not afford, they'd make a small deposit to hold the purchases and then they made monthly payments, which we subtracted from the amount due. On the due date, the customer presented the balance, which was posted on a specialized register, and we gave the customer the merchandise. Stored in a huge back room, the laid-away inventory was sorted by number, but we constantly had to organize the boxes of clothing, shoes, and household items as merchandise was added or subtracted by customer deposits or pick-ups. It was my turn to do the tedious organizing in the back room.

As my hand reached for a box on a nearby shelf, my head snapped up. I heard a rough male voice on the other side of the wall. "Open up the cash register, bitch!" he ordered. I was listening to a robbery in progress, and there was no telephone in the storage area. "No," came Cora's firm reply. "I am *not* going to open the drawer." I knew she meant it.

I stood frozen in place, still reaching for the box. I knew what was about to happen. "Don't you know I will shoot you, bitch?" the voice said. "I ain't got all day! Now, stop playin' and open the damn drawer!" Cora sounded firm once again, and I began to feel afraid for her. "No, I will not," she said softly.

My choices were clear. I could safely remain hidden where I was or I could emerge from the doorway, open the register, save Cora's life, and hand over the money. In a heartbeat, the image flashed through my head—a gorilla pointing a pistol at my head and Terri grabbing me as I ran toward the locked door. In the next heartbeat, I decided to repay somehow what Terri had done for me. On the third heartbeat, before I could change my mind, I stepped out of the room with my empty hands raised over my head. The sweat-drenched, jittery gunman clutched the shiny .22 automatic in his right hand as he swerved the barrel of the weapon from Cora to the middle of my chest. "The bitch won't open the register," he complained, fumbling at the drawer with his left hand.

Without saying a word, I walked over to the counter and began removing cash from the register. I shoved the money at him. For some reason, he felt compelled to justify his violence. "Ma baby need shoes," he mumbled. "Christmas comin'." I just looked at him. When he turned to run up the stairs, I pushed the panic button. Cora was frozen to the same spot to the left of the register when the manager came bounding down the steps two at a time, asking us what had happened, just as we thought he would. He was happy to learn that I had not lifted the cash tray to hand over the large bills to the robber. Cora turned toward me and mumbled, "Thank you," and then tears ran down her trembling cheeks. She still stood in the same spot.

I was married by then and would soon graduate from college, so I quit the job a couple of months later. But, before I quit, I convinced the manager of the department store to hire my younger brother, Butch, as a porter to replace Walt. Butch was a cheerful, hard worker and everybody liked him. He needed the money, since he had been unemployed after his graduation from high school. In a few years, he would marry an elementary school teacher and become a troubleshooter in the computer division of the telephone company but, at that time, he was just a confused teenager on the brink of disaster. We worked different schedules, so I seldom saw my brother inside the four-story building.

One afternoon, the manager asked to speak to me privately. He started out by telling me what a good job Butch had been doing, but then he gave a ferocious tug on the hair at the crown of his head. "Listen," he said, "I have to fire him." "*What?* Why?" I protested. "An inventory of the shoe department showed recent losses from theft, and we found empty shoe boxes in the trash bins behind the building." They had carefully watched the shoe department and believed that my brother Butch had stolen at least one pair of men's shoes during the past week. I was furious. My brother was innocent! He had stolen nothing! My feelings were hurt that they would falsely accuse him like that. I was out of control and the manager could not calm me down.. "How can you possibly believe that my brother is the one who took the shoes?" I finally screamed at him. The manager looked down at the floor and he actually seemed to be embarrassed for Butch. "Lillian," he said calmly, "he's wearing the stolen shoes to work today." And indeed he was. Years later, I learned that he had also stolen the fancy dress and matching shoes that my younger sister had worn to her prom that month.

The manager did not know it at the time, but I was a thief, too. When I dropped out of college, I had incorrectly assumed that three years of college credits with a B-plus average and several years of experience as a cashier would enable me to get a decent full-time job. I was wrong. During my working life, I had counted at least three jobs I could perform without a college degree. They were telephone operator, bank teller, and cashier. The problem I encountered was that only *white* high-school graduates were allowed to perform these jobs, and I discovered this problem for the first time when I applied for vacancies in the three positions all over the downtown area of Washington, D.C. I had been living in the city since my birth, and I had ignored the racism that was flaunted in my face every day. When I showed up for interviews, I was told the vacancies had been filled, and yet the advertisements for them ran long after I was turned away. I was very bitter when I had to continue working at the same department store, full time now instead of part time.

Walter had decided to quit his own job in his first semester of law school. My husband's plan for gainful employment was to rent a taxicab by the week and drive it part time while he attended classes sporadically. The only problem with this plan was that he was a terrible cab driver. He did not care that his earnings were not covering the bills and we were mired in debt. The thefts from my cash register started out small, fueled by my irrational rage at being rejected by other employers in favor of white applicants. My thefts were facilitated by the will-call system, and I had a simple scheme. When customers came to pay installments, we posted that money and gave the customer a receipt showing their new balance. But, when a customer retrieved will-call merchandise, I gave them their merchandise from the will-call room and, later, pocketed the cash. This theft would be discovered only through a physical audit of the entire posting system, which occurred merely annually. I also made sure to take the money only when I worked shifts with other cashiers. I may have stolen thousands of dollars this way, rationalizing it because of the racism that had prevented me from obtaining better-paying employment. Mostly, however, I blamed Walter for quitting his job, for being an incompetent taxi driver, for never noticing that our lifestyle greatly exceeded our legitimate income, and for turning me into a thief again.

Growing up, we had all been petty thieves. Our parents did not give us any spending money, allowance, or gifts of any significance, and neither did any other adults. We all conspired to steal money from my mother's purse or wallet, which she usually kept hidden under lock and key. It was always stuffed full of cash, which she never bothered to count, and the trick was to snatch an amount that she would not miss. We had long, secret meetings in which we decided how to spend the proceeds and then how to divide them. The penalty for telling on any sibling was swift, harsh violence, followed by ostracism. I personally graduated to shoplifting Snickers candy bars—for a thrill—whenever I went grocery shopping for the family dinner. Only once, a woman shopper caught me stealthily slipping the candy into my coat pocket. "Put that candy bar back," she sharply demanded. I fixed her with a silent, cold stare, which I had mastered. She quickly looked away without saying anything to the cashier. I was ten years old.

Before I lost my faith, I described each theft in detail when I went to confession. We chose our outfits from huge bins of donated, secondhand clothes at the Catholic Church's Saint Vincent de Paul Society outlet. Mr. Riccioli, from down the street, donated our shoes. He repaired old shoes and gave us the pairs that customers failed to pick up. Our winter coats and hats and itchy green blankets came from the Army-surplus store downtown. Years later, I found mortgage papers that proved that my parents had mailed double- and triple-payment money orders to the bank, paying off their thirty-year mortgage in less than ten years. All the while, they told us that they could not afford decent food or clothing.

*Queen of the Beach, 1962.*

# Scene Thirteen

No, I didn't.

My inability to obtain a good job without a college diploma or a teaching certificate made me even more obsessed with making sure that I would teach in the D.C. public school system. When the curriculum at my college allowed student teaching, I was ready for the challenge. They made assignments geographically, based on residence, so my junior-high school posting was within walking distance of the new Northeast apartment I shared with my husband. When I reported for duty that first day, I had no idea that my dream would not come true.

The college required that I rotate through the classrooms of several different experienced teachers to observe them and then, toward the end of the semester, to teach their classes. After a year of creating lesson plans and learning how to educate seventh through ninth graders in the strict public-school curriculum, I was woefully unprepared for what I found. None of the classroom teachers used lesson plans. Students spent classroom hours reading aloud from shared textbooks or copying material from the blackboard. Books were not available for most of the students, and they could not take them home. The ones they had were ragged, torn, and filthy, with missing pages and covers. Most shocking, none of the students was reading even close to grade level. In order to teach them anything, I would have to know how to teach on an elementary-school level, but I had not taken any elementary-school teaching courses. Furthermore, I had no *desire* to teach on that level. It was much too boring and, thanks to my miserable childhood, I did not like being around young children. I was surrounded daily by students whom I could not teach.

One of the history teachers with whom I worked was particularly horrible and, from my classroom observations, I knew that he was incompetent. His entire teaching hour consisted of anti-white rants in which he mangled the facts of United States history. His hate-filled speeches left the students depressed and angry as they filed into the crowded school corridors.

Those corridors were an obstacle course for me. Due to my small size and my baby face, my fellow teachers and the administrators routinely mistook me for a junior-high student. They constantly stopped me, demanding to see my hall pass, and I was required to show my identification. However, my worst experience at the school did not occur in a classroom or hall, but in the teacher's lounge. While the teachers gathered there to eat lunch, complain about the administrators, and laugh at the "ignorant" students, I reluctantly met my assigned teachers there on a regular basis. One afternoon, the ranting history teacher was explaining a black-power theory to his rapt peers in the lounge. I could not take it anymore. As a history minor and a reader of history books on my own since the fourth grade, I knew that he had United States history dates and events terribly confused, but none of the teachers corrected him. Before I knew what I was doing, I blurted out, "You have the Civil War mixed up with the Revolutionary War, you fool!" I had not meant to offend him but, rather, merely to correct him. After all, in my family, this was an acceptable way to converse with my siblings. The man did not take the correction well.

Incoherently screaming something, he lunged across the table and reached for my throat. I stood my ground. As he turned over the chairs that separated us, I gave him an evil stare. A trio of teachers grabbed his torso and arms and dragged him away from me. I finally figured out that he was bellowing the same sentence over and over again. "She called me a fool," he hollered. "She called me a fool!" When the teachers restraining him realized that I had a clear shot at the door, they yelled at me, "Leave the room!" I gladly fled into the corridor, shaking my head in wonder.

My next worst experience occurred inside a classroom about a month later. One of the students was a six-foot-tall, stoop-shouldered, well-dressed seventh grader who read on a second-grade level. I had obtained picture books on his reading level from the library so that he could understand the plot of the Shakespeare play that the class was required to study. Although he was passive and very sweet and polite, he often got bored and, when he got bored, he babbled. His babbling was worst when I turned my back to write on the board, which was often, because the lack of English grammar textbooks required me to do a lot of blackboard writing. I routinely had him sit about two feet away from me and, when he started up, I recognized his voice and asked him to be quiet so the rest of the class could concentrate on their studies.

Usually, the special attention calmed him down, but on this particular day, nothing worked. He emitted a steady stream of mindless chatter. "I wish I knew what that word meant," he might start saying. That would lead to, "I wish I were a man," and, "I wonder why I'm not smart, too." Babbling on and on, he'd say, "What does this word mean? How do you say that word?" Without realizing what I was doing or saying, I suddenly whirled around, holding a chalk-filled eraser in my right hand. "I told you to be quiet!" I screamed at him, smashing down the eraser squarely on the top of his head. I only knew what I had done when I saw the evidence—a perfectly rectangular print of chalk on the top of his short-cropped crown. I could even see the spaces between the felt strips, which were clearly visible. In amazement, I stared at the eraser, still gripped in the offending right hand, and so did every silent student in the classroom. My head swiveled from the eraser to the startling white imprint on the boy's head. Slowly, I became aware that the child was moaning. "You hit me," he said softly, over and over. "You hit me with the eraser." After he said this a few times, his mouth stayed open and he struggled not to cry. I reached over to him and gently smudged the perfectly straight lines that the blow had left on his hair. "No, I didn't," I lied. Then, I calmly turned my back on him and continued to write on the board.

That night, I decided that teaching junior-high school in Washington, D.C. was definitely not for me, even though the principal of the school had offered me a teaching job after graduation. All semester, at the end of each day of student teaching, I had been throwing myself on my bed, fully dressed, in a funk of depression. I already knew that my dream was slowly slipping away from me.

I made my decision to attend law school as the result of an utter fluke. On some basic level, I had always assumed that Walter was much smarter than I was. After all, in high school, he took Latin, was close to the top of his class, and all his friends were smart, and then he graduated from an Ivy League men's college. In fact, I did not know anybody smarter or better educated than my husband was. Although I knew a little Spanish and French, I thought it far more impressive that Walter knew Russian and Latin.

I had never met an attorney, and I viewed the profession as some sort of super-secret men's club with passwords and magic formulas for solving complex societal problems. Walter just wanted to be a lawyer so that he could avoid the Vietnam War draft. It showed. Walter hated law school, had made no friends there, and was bored by every class he took. As his four years of law school drew to a close, it was crucial that he improve his grade point average by doing well on each of his final examinations, since he had already been on academic probation for a year. But, whenever he opened a casebook to study, he fell asleep within ten minutes. One night, I could stand it no longer. I grabbed the book from his drooping hand and declared, "I will read it to you." Accustomed to reading to my younger siblings and to the junior-high students, I was pretty good at it. By the time I finished reading the first judicial opinion to Walter, I was in love, and there would be no turning back. I had found my new career.

The judicial opinions were  stories but, even better, they were problem-solving, conflict-resolving processes using legal precedent, history, and reasoning.  It would explain everything for me and I could be a part of it. Howard University Law School admitted black women like me, so all I had to do was to make sure that Walter graduated from law school, and then it would be my turn. I could spend three years learning these wonderful stories about esoteric problems. Somehow, I would memorize legal rules and, one day, I could be an attorney. Instead of *teaching* people, I could solve their problems using a system based on reasoning. A nobler calling could not exist. I couldn't wait to enter law school and begin a brand new life. If Walter—a man who never wanted to be a lawyer and who never met a problem he could solve—could become a lawyer, then I could, too. The casebooks proved it. Walter fell asleep as I silently devoured the rest of the  casebook. Then I started on the  next one as he snored softly next to me. Howard University was the only law school I applied to and, fortunately, they accepted me.

# Scene Fourteen

### Perhaps to Pray

I stood in the middle of the aisle in Notre Dame Cathedral, daydreaming about *War and Peace* and *The Hunchback of Notre Dame*, when Walter cried out, "Look who it is!" I was in my twenties, and it was my first trip to Europe. My husband and I had spent a week in London, and this was our second day in Paris. On a leisurely stroll in the middle of a cloudy spring day, we had taken three hours to explore the outside perimeter of the church, using a thick guidebook to enhance our appreciation of the pitted walls, flying buttresses, and gargoyles. We had saved the best part—the interior—for last.

When we entered the old church, a strong shaft of sunlight suddenly illuminated the nave. The rose window fractured the light into jewels. We had finished one side of the interior and were slowly working our way toward the other end when Walter spotted her. It was Penny, the reason we had taken the trip. Though Penny was our neighbor across the hall, we had not seen her in several months. She had not changed. Her immense, six-hundred-pound bulk was covered in a shapeless purple tent dress. On her naturally red, thick, glossy hair sat a straw hat. Perched at a rakish angle, it emphasized the purple eye shadow, milky white skin, and blood-red lipstick of our fortyish neighbor. In spite of her girth, Penny almost jogged toward us before she came to a stop in stages, her flesh never quite ceasing its watery motions under the billowing fabric.

We had performed cat-sitting duties for her temperamental Persian for three successive springs while Penny toured Europe on two-week jaunts. When we first met her, Walter and I were both looking forward to traveling outside the country, but we could not afford it then. Penny brought back a gift for us from each trip, but what we treasured most were her descriptions of her adventures and of the wonderful old cities that we had merely read about or seen in movies. Penny was very nervous as she called out to us. "Hi, Lillian," she said. "Hi, Walter. What a surprise to see you here! Pardon me, but I am in a terrible hurry." Clutching a camera in her dimpled fist, she was snapping photographs of the interior of the cathedral so rapidly that the flash attachment winked like a sparkler on the Fourth of July.

I had come to admire Penny greatly. In spite of her size, I imagined her to be a learned and sophisticated observer of the cultural and architectural wonders of Europe. My imagination had placed her in the pews of Notre Dame in the morning and returned her for live performances of liturgical music in the evening. She always sat quietly, closed her eyes, and became transported in her own mind to a much earlier century, before the revolutionaries pillaged the cathedral and used the apse for a place in which to cook food for the poor. The ceiling had remained charred for two centuries. Penny had inspired me to choose London and Paris, her two favorite cities, for our first trip to Europe.

"What's the matter, Penny?" I asked, curious about her state of mind. I wondered why she was in such a hurry. Hadn't she just arrived inside the most beautiful building I had ever seen? I considered that maybe she was in trouble, and we could help her out. "Oh, nothing is wrong, Lillian," she said, waving a flabby arm in a gesture of dismissal. "It's just that the last time I was here, the bus was on a tight schedule and I did not get to spend much time inside this church, so I forgot what it looked like. This time, I decided to take photographs so I can remember. But the bus is ready to pull off and I'm afraid they might leave without me." Penny hurriedly snapped two more photographs and then looked over her shoulder. Following her gaze, I spotted a knot of American tourists—about thirty of them—rushing to buy souvenirs in the gift shop and feverishly pressing buttons on cameras so that they could remember. Their tour guide waved frantically in their general direction and pointed with a pained expression at the watch strapped to her left wrist. It was time for Penny to go.

So *this* was how Penny visited Europe, crowded on a mammoth bus with other Americans and rushed from place to place like a child. I tried to resurrect old conversations with her so that I could determine the answer to a question that had bothered me since she had appeared inside Notre Dame that day. Had Penny *intentionally* misled me into thinking that she was an intrepid traveler who risked her life for beauty, or had I created a story for myself by ignoring the parts of her stories in which she mentioned tour guides and yellow buses? As Penny's gargantuan thighs mounted the bus steps and disappeared into the throng, I concluded that I would never know the answer to the question. I began instead to imagine the hunchback lumbering toward the altar behind me, while Walter watched the yellow bus pull out into rush-hour traffic, leaving us behind—perhaps to pray.

# Scene Fifteen
## Pregnant

I developed a strange obsession during my pregnancy, which I had kept secret from my husband. Having fallen out of love with him over the course of our marriage, I had been ambivalent about staying married to him while raising a child. Although I knew Walter in high school, we had become lovers while he was on academic probation from college. I did not know it at the time, but he had been forced to take a year off from college because his grade point average was so low. He told me that he was just taking time off from classes to earn money for his next year's fees. We were married the summer of his college graduation, and I moved into his one-bedroom apartment in Northeast Washington, D.C. Having rescued me from my miserable childhood, he was my knight in shining armor, and I was crazy about him. At the time of the wedding, I was attending D.C. Teachers College full time and working part time as a cashier, while Walter was working full time and planning to attend law school full time in the fall. We had been married eight weeks when Walter told me the bad news. He could no longer hold down a job while he attended law school, so I would have to quit college and get a full-time job so that he could graduate from law school on time, in three years.

The main reason we had become lovers was that he provided me with my first experience with oral sex. He had stripped off my panties while I stood in the downstairs hallway of my parents' house. As they slept soundly on the floor above us, I writhed around on the floor in the grip of a sexual fugue that I was powerless to control. In other respects, his amorous skills were prodigious, but he had a hesitant, gentle touch that seemed passionless and feminine to me and that I found slightly repellant. He expressed his sexual desire obliquely and I sometimes found it annoying or impossible to read the subtle signals that accompanied his arousal and need for sexual contact. In other words, I ignored him a lot.

I regarded his inability to work while attending law school as a betrayal and a cruel trick of fate. Although I dutifully dropped out of school and worked full time as he suggested, I also hoped that my response would change and that, in the near future, I would once again be crazy about my husband. This was not to be. Things got worse. Walter got kicked out of law school for a year due to poor grades and, by the time he graduated, our marriage was on the ropes, although it would be several more years before we separated and divorced. Meanwhile, out of curiosity, I decided to get pregnant. It was impossible for me to imagine what my child would look like or what kind of personality the child might have. I would give Walter the chance to play the role of father. If I did not like the way things developed, I would leave the child with him or raise the child by myself. With this level of confusion and ambivalence, I was naturally a nervous wreck during my pregnancy. I told my new lover, Herman, that I was pregnant three weeks before I informed Walter of the fact that he was going to be a father. I finally informed him of the good news over the telephone as I sat fuming in my office over something that he had done or failed to do that morning.

During my pregnancy, I pretty much ignored Walter while I pursued a bizarre sexual relationship with Herman, a shorter, darker, better educated version of my first Walter, Walter Lamb. We soon established a pattern.

Herman and I worked within a short distance of each other, and I would telephone him and ask when he was available, then I left my office five minutes before the appointed time. As soon as he opened his office door, we pounced on each other, kissing and tearing at clothing. Regardless of the size of my swollen belly, I was able to yank his trousers down with alacrity. Then, I dropped to my knees and allowed my oral craving to take over. Though sexual intercourse consisted of premature ejaculations and whispered apologies, Herman was a considerate, sweet, tender lover and the ideal recipient of oral ministrations. He moaned and writhed with every flick of my tongue and caught his breath when my hand caressed his shaft to join it to my mouth. As I slid toward his fragrant testicles, he stumbled backward to the sofa in utter joy. He let me slobber all over his pubic area and pretended not to notice when I noisily brought myself to orgasm over and over via my oral fixation on his privates. "Please come in my mouth," I whispered to him softly when I was completely exhausted from my own activity. "Please, come on my face. Please, now." He dutifully complied, with a symphony of soft moans.

We kept up these meetings for months, until it dawned on me that I was in the grip of an obsession, unable to stop myself from making the calls. Though I promised myself that I would not call him, I broke my own promise several times. Finally, I wrote myself a coded note, which I taped to my desk lamp, six inches away from my face, so that I could remind myself of my promise. But I also ignored the note. One afternoon, a visitor to my office spotted the eight-by-twelve sheet of paper stuck on the lamp and asked, "What does LHA mean?" I nearly blurted out, "It means 'Leave Herman alone,' of course." Stopping myself just in time, I substituted some nonsense for the real sentence but, in that moment, I suddenly knew that the compulsion had run its course. I never called Herman again.

# *Scene Sixteen*

## A Cute Day

As I wrestled my suitcase from the conveyer belt, a blonde surfer dude rushed toward me, smiling broadly. "Need some help?" he asked, pointing to the huge brown tweed Hartman suitcase in my hand. I was not surprised at the offer. After all, it was a cute day.

The phenomenon of a cute day demonstrated clearly the arbitrary nature of life itself. Within an hour of forcing myself out of bed and beginning the rituals of dressing and primping, I could tell whether it would be a cute day or not. The occurrence of such a day bore no relationship to the amount of sleep that night, my general health, the style of my hair, my plans for the day, or my age. Cute days had been occurring with the same freakish frequency throughout my entire adult life. On a cute day, I could do no wrong.

It was July, and I had just arrived at LAX for a short stay with a girlfriend who lived in Hollywood, California. The surfer dude, in his twenties, would never imagine that he was flashing his best matinee-idol smile at a woman in her forties, and I knew that I did not look my age that day. In his flip-flops and sun-faded Hawaiian shirt, which was open to the waist, he looked too poor and too young to waste time on. "No, thanks," I said with a smile. "I have it." I was grateful for any offer of assistance in life, even if unneeded. "Nice suit," he nodded in appreciation.

It was not really a suit, but I had been complimented on the outfit and on my shoes several times during the trip from the East Coast. Because it was a cute day, it did not matter that I had picked out white cotton trousers and a mismatched white silk blazer for the flight. Black-and-white spectator pumps with four-inch heels, three gold chains, diamond stud earrings, and a sheer white blouse completed my simple travel ensemble. I had been surrounded by smiling faces and displays of good will all day. Good thing it was a cute day, because I had no idea where I was going to spend the night. I strode confidently out the sliding door into the cool desert night and looked for the taxi stand outside the arrival area.

My girlfriend had made it clear that I would not be spending the night at her house. She had loads of houseguests and complicated plans that did not include me, but it was too late for me to change my airline reservation without a penalty and great inconvenience. Still, I had not made arrangements for my first night. With plenty of clubs around Hollywood and the Los Angeles area, I could spend the night drinking and dancing or, if worse came to worst, I had a pile of cash and a few credit cards that I could spend on an outrageously expensive hotel room in the city. Anyway, I loved staying in hotels and I was looking forward to an adventure. When I figured out what was up, I would call my friend so that she would not worry about me.

A taxi sat right under the sign, empty. Surprised that there was no queue, I leaned in through the open passenger window and asked, "Are you available?" The shadowed driver leaned over as if to answer my question but he said nothing, staring with such intensity at my chest that I looked down to see what he was looking at. Too late, I realized that the combination of the angle of my lean, a button that had worked its way loose on my sheer blouse, and a lacy bra had revealed most of my breasts to the driver. He started a conversation with my nipples. "I just pulled up to start my shift," he said. "You were the first passenger out the arrivals door. What can I do for you, pretty lady?" Before I could stand up straight or reply to him, the driver had hopped out of the taxi and run to my side of the vehicle. As he reached for the Hartman, I got a good look at him.

He looked familiar, but I could not recall how I knew him. His narrow feet were shod in off-white pigskin suede. Like most men in Los Angeles, he wore no socks. The matching trousers were fine linen and his shirt was custom made. A twenty-four karat gold bracelet adorned a slim wrist and blonde hair fell over his high forehead and dark blue eyes.

His upper lip was too thin and his eyes bulged when he smiled, but he was tan, fit, and in his thirties. He was my kind of guy, even if he was white. I relinquished the luggage, and he flung it easily into the trunk as I told him to head for downtown Los Angeles. We had not traveled far when he stopped for a red light. He threw his arm over the back of the passenger seat and introduced himself as Mark Shales. "Do I look like Roddie McDowell?" he asked me as he grinned to reveal two rows of beautifully capped teeth. "People tell me all the time that I look like the actor Roddie McDowell. You know, from *Planet of the Apes*. Do you think I look like him?" So, *that* was why he looked familiar. I could not imagine any man on the East Coast asking me that question, but I had forgotten about the obsession that Californians have with the movie industry. He was waiting for a reply. "A little," I said with a straight face. "But you are *much* better looking."

As we approached the city, Mark asked me for the specific downtown address. I had skipped lunch on the plane and still had not figured out where I would spend the night. "I am really starving," I said with a smile. "What is your favorite restaurant in Los Angeles? Just drop me off there." I dug into my wallet to assemble the cash for the huge fare displayed on the meter. "What are you doing?" Mark demanded, staring at me in the rearview mirror. I stared at the back of his bleached-blonde head as he reached over to the meter and snatched it back to zero. "I'm taking you to dinner," he insisted. "And don't *even* think about paying any of the fare." I was not surprised. After all, it was a cute day.

We walked into a friendly, crowded restaurant where Mark was obviously a regular. By the end of the meal, I had confessed to him that I had no plans for the night, but that I was spending the next few days with my girlfriend. "Perfect," he smiled. "You can spend the night at Laguna Beach with me!" He told me that he lived alone in the hills above the beach, about an hour's drive up the coast from where we were, and I was welcome to spend the night. He was lonely and seldom had guests, and he would be delighted if I accepted his offer. "No strings attached," he said, adding that he expected "nothing in return." In fact, he said, it would be his "utter pleasure to be of assistance to such a beautiful woman"—by whom he meant me. He was most concerned about my girlfriend and insisted that I call her to let her know that I was safe, regardless of my decision about his offer. Before we left the restaurant, I called her from a public telephone and told her that I had hooked up with some old friends in the city. I assured her that I would be at her house in the morning and I hung up quickly so she could not tell that I was lying about my evening plans. She would not have approved and I was in no mood for an argument. Besides, I had never been to Laguna Beach and I was looking forward to seeing his house in the hills.

Before we could leave for the beach, Mark had to return the taxi to the rental agency and retrieve his car from their premises. This task we accomplished in an urban-decay style garage that looked like it was the set of a situation comedy. It was filled with gasoline fumes and grimy immigrants who appeared to be pleased to see us. Mark's automobile was a red Italian sports car that barely had enough trunk space for my suitcase. He put the top down and we roared along the Pacific Coast toward the unknown. The house turned out to be a one-story building that clung precariously to the side of a mountain—*not* a hill. Californians make that mistake all the time. I had already discovered that a place in the "Berkeley Hills" is likely to be on the side of a mountain, as is a house in the "Hollywood Hills" and, sometimes, even one in "Beverly Hills." Below his house, at the base of the cliff, silver-tipped waves crashed against boulders in a ceaseless attempt to grind them into sand. Picture windows gave the illusion that the house was suspended in space. Mark removed his shoes before entering the house. Following him, I tripped and almost fell on my face.

Looking down at my feet, I saw that the entire floor was constructed of used wine corks, which were wedged tightly together to form an uneven surface that stretched to every corner of the house. I bent down to slip off my high-heeled shoes so that I would not stumble again. When I looked up, Mark was pointing expansively to the cork-lined floor. "Do you like it?" he asked, with the expectant air of a toddler who had just smeared grape jelly on his bedroom walls in a pattern that made sense only to him. I pasted a smile on my face. "I've never seen anything like it," I said truthfully. "Where did all the corks come from?" Mark was happy to explain that he had arrangements with bartenders all over the coast. "It took me years to finish the floor," he said, "but the work is not complete yet." He pointed proudly to a corner where I saw corks marching up the far wall. This quirky fellow was getting more interesting every minute.

"Please, make yourself at home," he insisted. "I'll sleep in the guest bed and you can have mine, because it's more comfortable." He pointed to a futon in the corner. How sweet. Wordlessly, I stepped toward him and kissed him very slowly on the lips, tongue, and teeth. He tasted good, and his expensive cologne was worth every penny. I walked to his bed and sat down. "Come here," I whispered. He did, twice. Then he licked me and kissed me into oblivion.

In the morning, he drove me and the big suitcase down the mountain and to Hollywood. As he set the suitcase on the steps, we promised to keep in touch and he climbed quickly into the tiny red car. We never talked again. When my girlfriend opened her front door, he gave a big wave and sped off. She stared at the car as it careened around the corner, and then she looked sternly at me. "What was *that* all about?" she asked, grabbing my shoulder. I bent to pick up the tweed bag and shrugged my shoulders as I walked through her front door. "Well," I replied, smiling, "yesterday was a cute day."

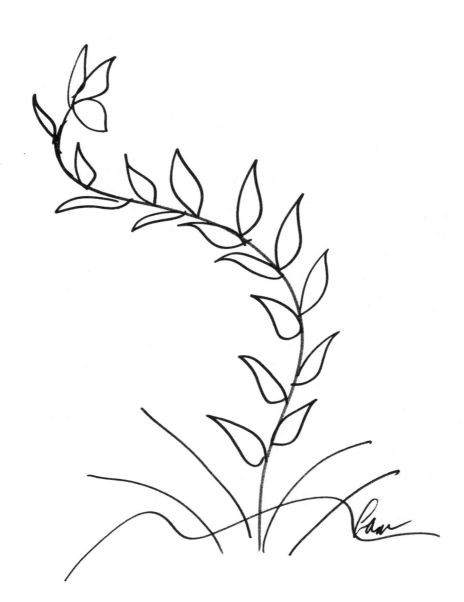

# Scene Seventeen

## Criminal Law

One of the strangest cases I handled in private practice started with a telephone call from Hiram, a stuttering, lanky police officer who had been a high-school friend of my older brother. When Hiram began to explain that his wife had been arrested for kidnapping, I recalled the newspaper account. A woman had abducted a newborn infant from a local hospital and brought the baby home to her husband. She told him that she had given birth suddenly, without him, and the proud father had arranged a party to celebrate the birth. While he was making the preparations, the father recalled seeing a newspaper photograph of the infant who had gone missing from the maternity ward and that's when he realized that his newborn daughter looked exactly like the child in the newspaper story. A police officer, he had his own wife arrested immediately.

On the telephone, Hiram was distraught. I discussed the general facts with him and gave him an estimate of my fee, while an important part of my brain was busy assessing how dumb Hiram had to be, not realizing that his wife had not been pregnant and had not recently given birth to an infant, and that the baby was not his. Of course, I expressed none of these thoughts to the man who would pay my fee and, when I met the wife, I was glad that I had remained silent on these subjects. After settling on a payment plan with the husband, it was necessary to get the client released as soon as possible. Within three hours of the phone call, I was at the jail where she was held. Talking my way past about ten military-style police officers and guards, I finally was allowed to enter the stark, metal-furnished room where my client was detained.

Her hands were primly folded on the grey steel table at which she sat. With my hand stretched out for a handshake, I felt my eyes involuntarily bulging when I stepped toward her. Her bushy, straightened hair was parted down the middle of her large, perfectly round head and pigtails brushed each shoulder. Her cherry-red lipstick covered thick, sensuous lips that were stretched to their limits in a big, goofy smile. Mascara and green eye shadow adorned the enormously wide, cow-like eyes, and her milk-chocolate cheeks were shiny with clownish rouge. She wore a frilly, light pink checkered maternity outfit that was trimmed in lace, which strained over her distended belly. She looked like a happily, gloriously pregnant woman in her seventh month. Her husband had warned me that her belly had gradually enlarged during the past nine months and that, when she had announced that she was pregnant, he had believed her. Seeing her, I understood why. Before I sat down across from her, I also saw that my client was seriously mentally ill. She was the only person in the room who was smiling.

Because the baby was unharmed and because the client's husband was a police officer, she made bail easily and I was able to get her released and examined by a psychiatrist. Over the next few months, I met with her quite frequently. As her belly shrank, she emerged as a childish yet voluptuous girl-woman, who wore flowery print dresses above her knees and a smile that seemed glued to her perfectly round face. She had precipitated a kind of hysterical pregnancy, becoming bloated with nothing inside. This childless woman, who had a history of miscarriages, had convinced herself that the baby she had stolen actually belonged to her.

With a nursing background, she had found it easy to obtain employment in the maternity ward. Then, all she had to do was wait for the ideal baby, who looked like her and her brown-skinned husband. Sitting in a wheelchair with the baby in her arms, she waited for someone to push her and the baby out of the hospital doors as she told nearby employees that her husband was coming to get her. After picking up his wife and the stolen baby from the curb, the policeman father took several days to realize that the kidnapped infant was in his own home. His wife's answers to his questions about the baby had not made sense and, finally, he called the authorities to report the location of the missing infant.

Eventually found not guilty by reason of insanity, my client was involuntarily committed to a mental institution. On the day she was committed, I had a doctor's appointment scheduled but, rather than requesting a postponement, I showed up in court early. I had a throat infection that, for several months, had been misdiagnosed as an allergic reaction and a mere sore throat. I am one of those rare patients who does not get an elevated temperature with an infection, and my throat does not swell or get red, either. A blood test is the only means of diagnosing the condition accurately and, by the time I had the blood test, I was very sick. I could barely stand up and I could not talk above a whisper.

I asked the judge if I could submit the written plea agreement into the record without reading it aloud but he refused my request. Consequently, while my client stood beside me grinning goofily as usual, I whispered into the record the four pages of facts and psychiatric findings that would send her to an insane asylum for an indeterminate length of time. The next day, on powerful antibiotics and bed rest, I was under orders not to use my voice at all. For two weeks, I communicated with the world via yellow legal pads.

My criminal law career began the summer of my second year in law school. I had successfully applied for a summer job as a student attorney in the United States Attorney's Office in Washington, D.C. Since the District is not a state, the federal prosecutor's office works with the local Metropolitan Police Department of D.C. and other law enforcement agencies—such as the Park Police Force and the FBI—to prosecute local felony and misdemeanor cases. The office was understaffed and, as a result, I was able to function as a full-time Assistant United States Attorney in many areas, including misdemeanors, serious felonies, and grand jury investigations. By the end of that summer, my fifteen-hour work days and intuitive grasp of criminal law had paid off. In just a few months, I had memorized the entire U.S. Attorney's Office Training Manual, which listed the elements for proof of each criminal offense in the jurisdiction, and I had mastered the new national computer system that tracked offenders by aliases, date of birth, and charges.

I was working on an ongoing, complex grand jury investigation of a serial rapist, so the executives in the Office decided to extend my appointment so that I could continue this work until November, the end of my first semester in my third year. I was in heaven. The only hitch was that, early on, an executive had informed me that the Office had a policy of hiring prosecutors only from Ivy League law schools—and Howard University was *not* an Ivy League law school. As a result, they made it clear that I should not bother to apply for a position as an Assistant U.S. Attorney after graduation. I did not remind them that this Ivy League policy was racist, since those law schools routinely refused to admit black women applicants, but merely asked whether there was anything else I could do to get hired. The answer was that maybe I could clerk for a judge, as a year or two as a clerk might make a difference. They promised to write a letter of referral to any judge I chose for my application process.

I did not waste any time. I went down the list of every black judge on the Superior Court bench. I figured that there was no point in wasting my time with the white judges, since I had never known a white judge to hire a nonwhite clerk unless they were friends with their relatives. I sent my resume and a cover letter to each black judge and sent my list of judges to the Office with a request that they send a letter of referral to each one. Then, I waited for responses from the judges—and possible interviews.

By the end of my second year of law school, I had quit my job as a technical copy editor, which I had held since graduating from college. When I graduated from college, I was unemployed and devastated. Although I easily could have obtained a certificate to teach in the D.C.

public schools, I knew that the work would bring me a life of misery. I never contemplated teaching in white private schools  because I still felt strongly that the black community somehow needed me. Graduation meant that cashiering was over, but we had bills to pay. Again, I applied for positions advertised in newspapers. An interview with a white alumnus of my college landed me a copy-editing position at the publishing arm of the American Academy of Sciences. She had taken a chance and hired me as her first nonwhite technical copy editor, based solely on our shared alma mater. Of course, she had attended D.C. Teachers College when it was segregated, when white students attended classes in the Wilson Building and black students attended in the Miner Building, several blocks away. Working for her, I edited manuscripts and did layout for the *Journal of Geophysical Research* and *Radio Science*, two scientific journals that published physics and higher math research work from scientists all over the world. I fantasized about getting a master's degree and teaching in high school or college and, shortly after starting to work as a copy editor, I was admitted to George Washington University's master's program, but I was not happy there, either.

After a few years, I was able to quit my technical copy-editing job when Howard University Law School offered me a part-time job in the legal writing program. This program was a sort of remedial step, by which first-year students  learned to read legal opinions and write briefs, or summaries, of those opinions. When I returned to law school after my hiatus with the U.S. Attorney's Office, I was promoted to head of the program and, when I graduated, the Law School offered me a full-time position.

Meanwhile, I received only one response to the solicitations I sent to my list of judges. It was a summons to be interviewed at five o'clock one evening in chambers. The black female judge happened to be the speaker at my college graduation several years earlier, and I had seen her on the bench several times during my work in the Office. She was the only judge on the entire court that I had any connection to and I was optimistic and happy to hear from a woman who I thought was beautiful and sophisticated. Middle-aged and childless, she was married to an attorney who had been a prosecutor. She ran a strict courtroom and had a reputation as a very formal person in chambers. I knew that, as a black woman, she had to maintain a professional demeanor at all times, and I respected her for what others might describe as rigidity. Short, plump, and brown-skinned, she wore a wig of straight hair and a cosmetic mask that included concealer, mascara, heavy rouge, and smeared lipstick.

When I was kept waiting outside chambers for an hour before the bailiff opened the door to admit me to the judge's perfumed presence, I began to suspect that something was amiss. In her black robe, the judge sat behind her massive oak desk and applied more makeup. I waited for her to speak first. "Be seated," she ordered in her fake British accent as she pointed to the vacant chair in front of the desk. Slowly, she put the lipstick and mirror away in her top drawer, which she banged shut. I was really worried. "I have two things to tell you, young lady," she sneered. "The first is that the United States Attorney's Office will never be allowed to dictate who shall serve as my law clerk. I am offended by their letter, and it was a blatant attempt to manipulate me. The interference by the United States Attorney's Office means that I will *not* consider you for the position. I will, however, take up the matter with them at a later date." She threw papers across the desk and I stared dumbly at her blood-red manicured nails as they flew through the air. "The second thing that I have to tell you is that, even before I read your papers or the reference from the Office, I had decided that I would never hire a female law clerk again. My present clerk, a woman, has disappointed me greatly. Now, she is pregnant—and she is unmarried. I decided that, given her situation, I would allow her to extend her clerkship, but I will *never* take the chance that such a situation will occur in my chambers again."

While the judge continued her bitter tirade, I sat in front of her, mute, but I was struck deaf, unable to hear any more of it. As the judge angrily ranted at me, I mused that she must have been terribly hurt and embarrassed by the law clerk's pregnancy, especially given her own childless marriage. I wondered whether she had bothered to ascertain that I was already married, and I wondered whether she cared.

The angry, bitter old woman took about an hour to spew forth the venom that she had stored up for me. "What do you have to say for yourself?" she demanded, finally signaling that the "interview" was over. "I apologize for the wording in the reference letter," I managed to say. "I am sure they did not intend to pressure you in any way." When she excused me, I stumbled out of her chambers. Trying so hard to hold back my tears of anger and disappointment, I could barely see. Without having had the chance to mention the commencement speech, I had just been rejected by the only judge I wanted to clerk for.

When I left the courthouse, I was so devastated that the judge's bailiff caught up with me and insisted on driving me home. I mumbled my address and got in the car for the five-minute drive to our new apartment in Southwest, just so that I would not have to argue with the bailiff. I knew that he meant well and I did not want to take it out on him. Staring out the window on the passenger side of the car, I did not say one word during the ride home, just tried to swallow the big lump in my throat. Then, I stumbled out of the car and ran to make sure he did not see the falling tears.

As soon as I was sworn in to the D.C. Bar, the United States Attorney's Office hired me anyway, without any judicial clerkship experience, probably to spite the judge. We figured that she had never gotten a reference letter from the Office before and that she might have thought it was somehow unethical. I was probably the first black law student who had ever spent the summer and fall before graduation doing the work of a prosecutor in the Office. A few days after my start date as an Assistant United States Attorney, one of my fellow prosecutors approached me with a smile, obviously intending to strike up a friendly conversation. "Hey," shouted Rhett, a tall, freckled redhead. "I heard a rumor that you got hired just because you have a great pair of legs." He grinned, staring at me, while engaging in what he thought was a little harmless flirtation. "Well," I said, staring him back in the face. "I don't care why I was hired. All that matters is that I'm here now!" I walked away from him, looking over my shoulder.

# Scene Eighteen
## The Republican

It was time for the cornrows to come out. Several weeks earlier, I had been seized by the need to tangibly express my blackness to the world at large, spending eight hours and too much money to have over two-hundred plaits done in my shoulder-length hair. Unfortunately, it was a disaster. The braids were so tight that the hairs had begun to pop out of my scalp along the hairline around my face. As soon as I looked in the mirror, proffered by the amiable hairdresser, I knew it was a terrible mistake. The braider mistakenly thought that each of the approximately two-thousand beads that I brought to the shop actually belonged in my hair, so a huge variety of colors and shapes randomly decorated the braids. The result was a bizarre assortment of plaits in varied sizes and widths. This colorful headdress clicked and popped and tangled with a maddening constancy that made it impossible for me to sleep more than three hours straight. Everyone said that I would get used to the noise, pain, and assorted colors, but I felt more uncomfortable with the hairstyle every day.

So, when the United States Senate changed hands and the Democrats became the minority party, I used the new political landscape as an excuse to have the braids taken out. It was no longer a good idea to look chicly radical in 1980, so I sat in the basement of the Russell Senate Office Building while several Senate staffers undid my cornrows.

I had been a counsel to the Judiciary Committee for about a year but the Republicans were poised to control most of the budget and hiring of the Senate Judiciary Committee. We had all decided that it was time to make friendly with the Republicans, and we all tried to list all the Republicans we knew. Senator Joseph Biden's staff was not known for close Republican ties, and my closest Republican ties were in the group of black Senate staffers. About a dozen of us met informally but regularly in the restaurants near the United States Capitol building for happy hour, when we'd hold down a corner of the bar at Bullfeathers or similar spaces.

I had learned that the best way to succeed professionally was to organize a black group or become part of an existing one. Thus, when I was a prosecutor in the United States Attorney's Office in Washington, D.C., I had helped to form the Black Assistant United States Attorneys Association. I was also a member of the Washington Bar Association, the local affiliate of the National Bar Association, which had been formed early in the twentieth century when white attorneys in the American Bar Association had refused to admit black attorneys. And I was active in the Washington, D.C. chapter of the Howard University Law School Alumni Association, because I loved my alma mater.

As I thought about the Republicans I knew, I saw one of them hurrying down the hall outside the office where I was getting my hair redone. To the amusement of the group gathered around me, I shouted, "There goes one now!" Then I ran out of the room with my hair half done. The Republican I recognized was one of the black Senate staffers whom I had met at the happy hour gathering. Although I did not recall his name, I knew that he was a legislative assistant to Senator John Danforth. As a counsel to the Judiciary Committee, I had been recruited by the Chief Counsel, Mark, to provide expertise for criminal forfeiture hearings that Senator Biden held as part of the reform of the RICO (Racketeer-Influenced Corrupt Organization) statute. My responsibilities also included judicial nominations, constitutional amendments, abortion, and civil rights. Legislative assistants, on the other hand, usually handled matters requiring relatively little legal expertise. When I ran after the man in the hall, I planned to introduce myself to him and hoped that he would remind me of his name. I did. He said, "You probably don't remember my name. It's Clarence, Clarence Thomas."

Although I am not a coffee drinker, I invited him to have coffee in the Senate cafeteria. He accepted and we became buddies. It did not take me long to learn that my new friend was married, living with his wife and a young son of about seven years old. His friends in Washington, D.C. consisted of Republicans and his fellow Yale Law School alumni. A lonely, bitter alcoholic, he established a pattern within a few months of visiting my spacious, one-bedroom apartment whenever I allowed him to. He stayed for as long as it took him to drink most of the vodka, rum, wine, or beer that I happened to have on hand and, in that time, he transformed himself into an angry, vengeful, self-pitying mess, tearfully recalling his miserable childhood and the hardships that he had endured. Then, he drove home drunk, but without staggering or slurring his speech. His impaired state would be obvious only to someone who counted his drinks and measured the prodigious amount of alcohol that he consumed over the course of the evening. His self-pity, searing anger, and alcohol intake were not shocking to me, because I had been drinking with black men like him since my freshman year in college. In law school, my best buddies were a group of about eight drunks who gathered in the student lounge every afternoon and took up a collection. After passing the hat (a fashionable fedora, usually), a volunteer made the obligatory run to the liquor store down the street, and then we spent the next two hours drinking from plastic or paper cups while we debated philosophy, religion, politics, and deprived childhoods with varying degrees of sobriety.

The new Republican majority in the Senate did not result in tremendous changes for the Judiciary Committee and none of my friends was fired. The general atmosphere on the Hill, however, changed so gradually to a conservative, moralistic one that it took a while to register. Of course, my personal life was being so thoroughly transformed that it eclipsed my professional one. In the midst of a divorce from the man I had married more than twelve years earlier, I was determined to get custody of my young daughter, Mitch.

She attended Capitol Hill Day School, thanks to Mark, my boss on the Committee. Mark's young son was at the private school and Mark had recommended it when my smarter-than-me four-year-old daughter informed me that she was "not going back to that school," Southwest Montessori, which I had chosen primarily because it was only two blocks away from my apartment. It was also a majority black private school, which was a big plus for a woman who wanted her daughter to have a firm racial identity. And it went through sixth grade, so I would not have to think about moving her for a while. Unfortunately, my supremely rational daughter gave me about ten reasons why I should not force her to attend the school of my choice any longer. The most convincing was, "Mommy, I have to fight the girls every day." The teachers blamed the fights on my spoiled daughter, who blamed the other students for teasing her about her unusual skin color and hair. Mitch's second-most convincing reason was, "Mommy, the teachers yell at us all day." Indeed, they did—and it seemed that this was the only way they could control the rowdy classroom. While the other children were oblivious to the yelling, my daughter was accustomed to a very quiet home and she was offended by the constant barrage of shouted orders.

I was not really surprised at my daughter's decision. She was "tender-headed," as the black hairdressers would say. My daughter felt acute pain when her hair was braided tightly or pulled and, although her hair was soft and curly, it was too frizzy and bushy to leave out every day, and so it had to be kept short or get plaited. Since I could not bear the thought of cutting her gorgeous light brown curls, I kept them plaited so that she had about twenty long, loose braids cascading down her back. The problem was that her Southwest Montessori teachers thought that these loose braids were unkempt and, at least once a week, they forced her to sit between their knees for hours while they redid her hair, ignoring her yelps of pain. "Mommy, will you tell them not to comb my hair?" she asked. "They won't listen to me." But they would not listen to me either.

The divorce was generally amicable and I obtained joint custody of Mitch. Soon, I bought her father out of the house that we had purchased while I was pregnant with her.

Somewhere in the middle of this chaos, I was seated on the sofa in the apartment that I would soon vacate. Clarence had come to visit after work as usual and he was probably on his fifth beer of the evening. He was behind me as I held a conversation with him and, out of nowhere, he bent over the back of the sofa and planted an upside-down kiss on my lips. Before that instant, we had never hugged, held hands, or petted. But his kiss was sweet, soft, and passionate. This was trouble. "You are a wonderful guy and a relationship with you would probably be great," I calmly explained. "The only thing is, I have this rule. I never date or have a romantic relationship with a married man, and I never intend to. It is morally wrong and I could not stand the guilt of thinking or imagining for even five minutes that I was the cause of the possible destruction of a marriage between two people who had vowed to remain married for life."

None of this was true. It was my theory (based on experience, novels, television programs, and rumor) that married men with children did not usually leave their families for other women. More importantly, I had no intention of commencing a romantic, serious relationship with anyone at the time, especially a man. If I did decide to commence one, it would not be with a bitter, angry drunk who probably earned less money than I did.

Ever the gentleman, Clarence appeared to be heartbroken upon hearing my speech. He promised to get a legal separation from his wife, divorce her, get custody of his son, and pursue a serious relationship with me. In turn, I pretended to believe him. I also promised that I would put no pressure on him to do anything he did not want to do, and then I quickly changed the subject. Secretly, I was relieved that the problem was solved without drama, that he would not harass me in the future for sex, and that we could continue to be buddies. Then I promptly forgot about the kiss and the conversation, never imagining what would soon happen.

A few months later, Clarence was again in my apartment for drinks after work. He got my attention. "I did it," he said with a big grin. I had no idea what he meant. I smiled back brightly and said, "Did what?" With some hesitation, he explained that he had moved out of the apartment he shared with his wife and son and that he would soon be filing for a divorce. I was flabbergasted. "Why?" I asked. I had never met any of his family members and he had never met my daughter or any of my family members, and I was genuinely confused by his decision. "Don't you remember what you said about us?" he whispered. I was stunned. He had believed everything I told him, and he had assumed that he had removed an impediment to a romantic liaison. It was the sweetest, most wonderful thing that any man had ever done for me and, in an instant, I was completely won over.

Until that exact moment in time, I had entertained no sexual thoughts about Clarence at all. Indeed, I had no idea what he might look like beneath his clothes. I had seen him only in baggy, cheap suits and shirts, and I assumed that he had the flabby physique of the usual workaholic attorneys I knew. An intense curiosity about his physical self overwhelmed me. I unbuttoned his white shirt. It would be easy for me to satisfy my curiosity, create some fiction about my inability to proceed, and then, in a few minutes, apologize for teasing him and send him away as usual. He would be back with his wife and son in a few days and we could remain friends in spite of this little misunderstanding. In the end, we would laugh about it.

But the removal of Clarence's shirt revealed a steely, hairless chest and shoulders that were covered in coffee-bean velvet. There was no way I could let him go without licking and kissing that skin. My curiosity kicked in again, and I had to see the rest. To get this definition, Clarence had been lifting weights and working out at the gym for years. I knew this from my own years as a gym rat and from the muscle development of my ex-husband, who also lifted weights. Clarence ran long distances on a regular basis, so his entire body was velvet-covered cement. I had to touch all of it, immediately.

When Clarence's trousers came down, I got a huge shock. He had not been circumcised as an infant and he had developed complications as a young boy. The physician who performed the late circumcision had mutilated him. This disfigurement by scalpel had transformed the head of his penis into a large bulb with four distinct sides sitting on top of the shaft. The shaft was connected to the head by a ridged lip that protruded an inch beyond it all the way around, and this ridge had corners on it. The shaft was thicker than my wrist, and the head was even wider, but it came to a relative point at its end, like a flexible pyramid. The botched surgery had created a fantasy penis, and I could not wait to smell it, taste it, lick it, suck it, and get it inside me. It was eleven inches long when erect, and I seldom saw it in any other state during our relationship. Most importantly, Clarence was one of those fortunate men who remained erect after ejaculation. For him, intercourse ceased naturally only when he had exhausted himself into a near coma. This process took so many hours that Clarence was well-acquainted with the wonders of KY Jelly, which was entirely new to me. His semen tasted like apple juice, and his saliva tasted like honey.

Clarence was so fastidious that his frequent showers had caused the skin on his shoulders and back to flake and peel. When I introduced him to fragrant baths, he was delighted, and he was soon purchasing oils and luxuriating in the tub after a long day. The skin all over his body eventually became glistening and baby smooth. He never abandoned his running regimen, and he wore out the soles of his running shoes. One evening, I saw him applying glue to them. Instead of replacing his shoes when they wore out, Clarence coated the bottoms with special glue. When it hardened, he could keep running in them.

# Scene Nineteen

## Saving Them

She was late again. As I stood in the lobby of the Superior Court building, I scanned the teeming crowd for any sign of my client. It had been several weeks since our last court appearance, but we would be starting the jury selection the following week. Arguments on pretrial motions were set for this morning and I might prevail on the most important one—my request to use the abused spouse syndrome as the basis for self-defense. It would be a case of first impression for the District of Columbia. If the judge allowed me to use my expert-witness psychiatrist, we had a chance to win the murder trial. Two facts worked against us, however. My client had not been married to the deceased, and she had sustained no injuries during the deadly altercation. The prosecutor had made much of these factors in his written opposition, which I reviewed once more in between worried glances toward the entrance doors.

I felt both relief and worry surge through my nervous system when I spotted my client Abby running through the crowd. Yes, she had arrived and she was dressed in church clothes as I asked her to be. As usual, she looked like Aunt Jemima on steroids, minus the kerchief, although she was only twenty years old. The problem was that, in her arms, she carried her new baby. Amazingly, my client had conceived while pending trial for murder in the first degree. She spotted my frantically waving arms and shook the crying infant harder as she rushed toward me. As the shaking became more vigorous, the tiny bundle howled louder and I decided that I would explain shaken-baby syndrome to my client later. At the moment, we had to run to the courtroom upstairs. "I'm sorry I'm late, Lillian," she said. "I couldn't get nobody to watch him." I reached for the baby. "Give him to me," I insisted. "I know how to calm down a baby."

I gently took the baby from Abby and then I looked into his eyes for the first time. As soon as I touched him, he stopped crying and looked me straight in the face. It was love at first sight, and it was mutual. He was a miniature version of his mother, whom I would never describe as beautiful, but, to me, at that moment, Adam was the most handsome baby boy in the world. When we walked into the courtroom, I refused to relinquish him to his mother. He had sighed and fallen asleep when I placed him against my shoulder, and he slept in my arms as I argued and won every motion that I had filed in the case.

This would be my second murder trial. In the first one, I had represented Larry, whose codefendants described him as the leader of their Eighth and H Street Crew, or gang. The Crew had robbed a middle-aged neighbor as she walked home in the rain carrying groceries, and then they brutally beat her to death. Her body was discovered on a mattress in a garage in the alley and it was a bloody and gruesome crime scene. The teenagers blamed the robbery and murder on each other. I lost every pretrial motion, including the one to separate the Crew members for individual trials.

When I ventured down to the crowded lockup in the basement of the courthouse to meet Larry for the first time, he was singing a heart-rending rendition of Prince's "Purple Rain" at the top of his lungs. None of his fellow prisoners joined in, but nobody was trying to stop him from singing, either. A defense of mere presence was the only hope for this light-skinned, sophisticated, gangly teenager who towered over his codefendants at six-foot-four. In spite of many visits to the D.C. jail to prepare Larry for his trial testimony, I had never been able to persuade him to cry or even to pretend to cry on the witness stand. Was it pride, stubbornness, stupidity, or fatalism on his part? He refused to explain. A jury of his peers found Larry guilty on all counts and he received a long prison sentence. Many years later, when I presided over trials as a federal administrative law judge at the Securities and Exchange Commission, I watched in wonder as white men, who had been accused of mere securities fraud, sobbed on the witness stand. They would never serve a day behind bars.

The first time I saw Abby she was also in the crowded lockup downstairs, but she was not singing. Her entire body was shuddering with huge sobs. "Gimme outta dis place here, " she begged me. When I saw the tears running together at the base of her many chins, my first thought was, "We have a chance." And I had not even interviewed her yet. Abby was blessed with the ability to cry at will (a gift that I do not have). When the judge said, "I will lock you up again if you appear late even once during the trial in my courtroom, young lady," Abby's tears flowed. Standing at counsel table with her sleeping baby in my arms, I promised that she would be on time each morning. At that moment, I decided that Abby would become a "project."

My first project was my niece Karen, who was Chee Chee's second-born child. By the age of fourteen, Karen had been in and out of foster care for several years, beginning with her mother's first suicide attempt when Karen was a toddler. My husband had passed the bar, I was in law school, and I had no plans to have a child any time soon. She was cute and smart, so I decided to give the teenager a permanent home. Chee Chee was institutionalized and our two-bedroom apartment could easily accommodate Karen. I had read every book I could buy or borrow about adolescents, and I knew that it was important to establish reasonable rules, which Karen would certainly test, but I would be both flexible and fair. I drew up a list. After I had obtained legal custody of Karen, she and I went over the list. She was enrolled in a public junior-high school nearby, and I explained carefully to her that private school and college would surely be in her future. "No, I don't have any questions, Aunt Lillian," she said with a smile. "And the rules are fair." Fine, I could rescue her. It would be easy.

A week after our conversation, I came home three hours early and heard a strange man's voice coming from Karen's bedroom. "I thought you said it was cool!" he was shouting. A tall, handsome half-naked boy-man emerged and walked toward me. Trailing behind him was half-naked Karen, smiling sheepishly and mumbling an introduction. "Get out of here!" I said to the male, barely controlling my instant rage. "Don't ever come back. She is a *child*." I turned to Karen. "We have to talk," I snarled. After I gained control of myself, we had a really good talk. Less than a week later, Karen disappeared. I did not call the police, because I suspected where Karen might have run to.

Even though my younger sister Pat had told me that she had not seen Karen, I could tell—even on the telephone—that she was not being truthful. My husband and I went to the squalid neighborhood where Pat lived with her husband and small baby girl. Karen had always liked Pat, who was ten years younger than me. Sure enough, we had been on Ninth Street, Northeast less than an hour when we saw Karen darting into a nearby alley. She spotted the two of us and ran away from us quickly. "I am *never* going back to live with you!" she shouted loudly for the entire block to hear her. "Don't come looking for me again! Leave me alone. You are both squares!" I was torn between laughter and tears. My first project had not turned out well at all.

A few years later, my second project was my younger sister, Pat. The whole family knew that Pat's husband Ves was an abusive bully who had assaulted her several times since she married him when she was seventeen. Several times, after frantic calls to the police, Pat and her toddler daughter had moved out of the house she shared with him, but my sister always went back to more broken promises and more abuse. But this time, I decided, would be different. I knew that it would not be easy, but I could rescue Pat and her daughter.

She had called the police and they had arrested him. Pat promised me, my husband, the police, and the prosecutor that she would testify against him in the assault trial and that she would divorce him and sue for custody of her daughter. I believed her and I believed her promise that she would not contact him or tell him that she was living in the second bedroom of our apartment. Two days later, there was a loud knock on my apartment door. Looking through the peephole, I saw Ves's grinning face pressed up against the metal door. He was waiting patiently in the hall. "What do you want?" I shouted through the door at him. He continued grinning. "I know Pat is staying with you," he yelled. "She called me on the telephone and asked me to bring some of her things. I have them in a bag right here. I just want her to have her things...."

My sister stood in the living room, about ten feet away from me and close enough to have heard Ves. "Is that true?" I demanded. "Did you really call him and agree to that?" With a tiny smile of shame on her lips, she nodded. Without a clear thought, I felt rage at Ves for being so mean to her, and I felt rage at her for putting up with his abuse for so long. Planning to curse him out, grab the bag of clothes, and tell him never to show his face near me or my sister again because we would see him in court, I unlocked the door. As I reached for the doorknob to yank the door open, my husband caught my wrist. "Don't open the door!" he shouted. I was too strong for him and Ves was too fast. Within three seconds, Ves shoved the door wide open and pushed me aside. "Where is she?" he screamed in my face as his saliva spattered my chin. "No!" yelled Walter, who outweighed the younger man by fifty pounds and stood four inches taller. With both arms outstretched, Walter propelled himself and Ves out the door and then he quickly reached behind his back and slammed the door shut in my face.

I locked the door and peered out the peephole to get a closer look at Ves and Walter. Ves pointed a .44 Magnum revolver at Walter's head. Walter ran a zigzag pattern down the narrow hallway. Fueled by alcohol and rage, Ves pursued Walter. "I will kill you, man," Ves mumbled, sounding as if he was crying. "I swear, I will kill you!" When Walter flew down the nearby fourth-floor staircase, Ves abandoned the chase and made his escape by taking the elevator to the lobby.

When I called the police, they expressed no surprise at this latest scene in the escalating domestic-abuse drama, but they promised to look for the armed husband. My sister and I had a long conversation about the situation; I warned her that if she foolishly went back to him after this latest criminal act—and if she failed to testify—she could not use my home for a refuge again. Instead, I would gladly give her money for that purpose in the future. Pat dropped the charges the next day, went back to him, and never asked me for shelter or money to escape from him again. That project had not turned out well at all.

My mother initiated my third project via a midnight telephone call. "Hi, Lillian," she said. "I'm calling to ask you a big favor. Remember my oldest brother, Bill? He lived in Long Island, New York, and he died last year? Well, he has an adopted daughter, a cute little thing—Janet. She's your cousin…" I had a bad feeling. "Yes, Mama," I sighed, trying to prepare myself mentally for the worst. "Well," Mama continued, "she wants to leave Long Island and come to the District to find work." This did not sound good. "Yes, Mama?" I sighed again. "I told her she could stay here with me, at the house, until she got on her feet, you know. I'm lonely here by myself and none of you will move in with me. You know that, since Chee Chee had the baby she's been all depressed about it and they took her back to Saint Elizabeth's for stronger medications. I think they put her baby in foster care. And, you know I had to put your crazy brother Anthony out of the house, when he tried to kill me five years ago…." Was she trying to make me jealous? It was not working and it did not sound bad at all. "Yes, Mama," I said, smiling. "Well, Lillian, Janet is all packed and she already paid for her train ticket and she said goodbye to her mother and all her friends up there, but she can't stay here and she will be here tomorrow…."

This was bad news, indeed. "Why can't she stay with you, Mama?" My mother did not hesitate. "Well, she's a *real* nice girl but I'm used to being by myself and I never liked having other women around anyway, you know. And it's just too much stress. I got the sugar and the pressure now to worry about." This was *very* bad. "Tell her not to come, Mama," I begged. "Well, Baby, I can't do that," Mama said, calling me "Baby" as she always did when she wanted something really important from me. "I never did much for them," Mama continued. "And I don't want to disappoint her, she's so sweet. I told her she could stay here for two days and after that she could stay with you." So my mother had already committed me to a project. I had to be firm. "No, I'm not going to do it. I'm definitely not," I said. "Lillian," she countered, "I never ask you for anything and you have that big house all to yourself since you divorced Walter for no good reason at all. You should have stayed married to him. Even Mitch is hardly there. She spends so much time with her father, and she's always traveling somewhere, and she hasn't even gotten out of junior high school yet. Don't be selfish, Baby."

That was something, my mother calling *me* selfish. Anyway, I caved in and agreed to meet my cousin the next day. I felt sorry for her. Janet arrived in Washington, D.C. with a large purse that was crammed with junk, underwear, and makeup but no money, and the ragged clothes on her back. I promised to help her find a job and to let her stay with me until she got paid. Lucky for her, she had a dancer's body, a cute, horse like face, long straight hair, and light acne-scarred skin. She could wear my makeup and she looked good in my clothes.

After asking her a few questions and perusing the skimpy resume she had with her, I told my cousin how to get a job. "Tomorrow you will leave the house by eight AM, wearing these clothes. Go straight to Hecht's Department Store. Here is the address. Take the elevator to the credit department, on the top floor. They will have a vacancy because their employees—like all employees in retail everywhere—are stealing every day. When they catch the employee stealing, they fire them and they tell all the other retailers not to hire them. So, you go to the manager of the credit department and show the manager this resume. Tell them you are honest and that you will work any hours you get assigned. They'll hire you immediately." I felt good. Janet's problems were simple and, in no time, she would be on her own, my first successful project.

The next day, Janet took my advice and, to her amazement, she was hired on the spot. By the end of her third month in my house, I called her mother in Long Island and asked seriously whether her daughter had departed so quickly that she had forgotten to take her medication with her. Her mother told me to send her thirty-year-old daughter straight home. After she hung up, she called my mother, who gave me hell for being so mean. During her three months in my house, Janet made no effort to find other housing, had made no friends, and begged me to set her up on a date. I introduced her to a single male friend of mine. After a nice dinner, she asked for a ride to see his house. When they arrived, Janet ran into the bathroom, stripped off her clothes, and emerged to fling herself onto his bed. He was so puzzled that he ordered her out of the house and then he waited in the car to bring her straight back to me.

A week after the naked incident, my lover told me that, one time, when I was not home, Janet let him in my house. She asked him to wait on the sofa, ran up to my bedroom, changed into my shortest, tightest, skirt, left off her panties, and invited him to have a much better time with her than he could possibly have with me. He fled the house and did not return until she had left the city. Clearly, it was time for Janet to leave my house.

Getting Janet to leave would be easy. Being a true slob, she never picked up after herself and she despised housework. A woman cleaned my house every week, so all I did was to ask her to take a week off with pay, and then I took the problem to Janet. "There's a great deal of cleaning that must be done this week and the help is on vacation," I said. "We'll have to do it ourselves, so let's start with the kitchen tonight." We stayed up all night, emptying every shelf and drawer, removing the liners, and scrubbing every corner in the upper cabinets and under the sink. Then, as dawn broke, we replaced every plate, pot, and spoon. "That was great work, Janet," I said, putting away the sponges as I pulled out a brand new bottle of strong bleach. "Thanks for helping me out. Now, tomorrow, we can do the stove and the refrigerator and start on the laundry room and the big closets under the stairs." The next day, Janet moved out of my house. My mother called and cursed me out for being so evil and "treating that sweet girl like a slave." I did not bother to explain. A month later, Mama told me that Janet had moved back in with her mother in Long Island.

A week later, I got a dreaded midnight call from my mother. "Lillian," she said, "I have bad news." I heard her crying softly. "What is it , Mama?" I asked finally, starting to grind my teeth. "Well, it's Janet," my mother said. "You know she moved back home?" I sighed. "Yes, Mama, you told me that last week." My mother cried softly and finally said, "Well, they found her this afternoon in the backyard." She paused. "She killed herself. She was hanging from a tree." I could not comfort my mother. Was she feeling guilty? I could not tell. She was still sniffling when I laid the receiver softly on the cradle. No, that project had not gone well either, that's for sure.

On the first morning of the murder trial, I woke Abby extra early to make sure that her outfit, hair, and makeup were appropriate for her court appearance. Even though jurors sometimes wore jeans, tennis shoes, and tee shirts, they expected the accused to dress and act with respect for the criminal justice system. After the prosecution rested its case, it would be our turn to qualify the psychiatrist as an expert and to present self-defense evidence to the jury. The problem with our case was that the deceased had been stabbed several times with a huge knife while Abby did not have a scratch on her. Thus, I needed the abused-spouse syndrome to explain how she had become so terrified of the deceased that she could not leave the relationship and that her fatal attack was rooted in that terror, even though the deceased was unarmed.

Before the prosecutor rested his case, he made much of the fact that the deepest stab wound was inflicted on the deceased's back. Then it was our turn. The testimony of the expert went well, and then several family members described arguments, threats, and altercations that the deceased had initiated. Then, I needed the testimony of Abby to explain the stab wound to the back. Although I had prepared her to describe the blow, she was not being clear on the witness stand. She appeared to be confused. If she faltered, she could get destroyed on cross examination to the point where I could not rehabilitate her. It was the fine line I had to draw in witness preparation. With too much preparation, a witness sounds robotic and loses credibility. Instead, to be authentic, the words have to be *theirs*. But, without enough witness preparation, their testimony could be garbled, incoherent, and easily shredded on cross examination.

To protect Abby on cross examination, we would have to do a demonstration of each stab wound. She would play the dead boyfriend and I would play the killer, using a folded piece of paper in place of the murder weapon. The demonstration went well until we got to the final deep blow to the back. It had to be inflicted with the boyfriend facing Abby in a threatening fashion while Abby reached around his arm or shoulder to plunge the weapon home. Any other scenario would have her killing an unarmed man with his back turned, which would make any kind of self-defense harder to prove. I asked Abby to rush toward me as the deceased must have done, and I grabbed her shoulders and reached around her with my right arm to plunge the paper in her back. Abby had begun to sob as soon as the demonstration commenced and, by the time we finished up, I realized that she was whispering something in my ear. As we struggled in the well of the court, I pulled her mouth closer to my ear so I could figure out what she was saying. "I'm sorry, Lillian," she whispered. "I'm sorry, Lillian. This is not how it happened. This is not how it happened."

Great. What a fine time to tell me that we'd made a mistake. Was she feeling remorse for the first time? Was it all a lie from start to finish? When I heard the whisper, we were standing about ten feet from the judge's bench, six feet from the court reporter, and twelve feet from the prosecutor. But we were only a *foot* away from the first row of jurors! Had they heard what she whispered to me? I kept my face expressionless as I plunged the paper into Abby's broad back with all my strength. Her size was a problem for me and the deceased, as she was five inches taller than the boyfriend and she outweighed him by fifty pounds. In a flash, I put Abby back on the witness stand. The prosecutor did no damage on cross and I quickly rested our case. The jury returned a speedy verdict of not guilty. Abby and the baby stayed at my house for several more weeks. I never asked her what she meant by the whispers during the demonstration, and I still wonder whether the jurors heard what she said to me and chose to ignore it.

During their sojourn at my house, the baby began to talk and crawl. Soon, he began calling me "Mama" and following me around. An abusive parent, Abby was always slapping the baby in the mouth and slinging him around on a whim.

It was time for them to return to her mother's house on Robinson Place, Southeast, which was in an area that consisted of public housing, carry-outs, and empty lots. Several drug dealers and violent offenders whom I had represented lived in the area. Although I felt comfortable in the adjacent streets, it was difficult to convince my boyfriends to give me a ride when I went to pick the baby up for a weekend visit. If I traveled by bus, Abby always made sure that some older children stayed with me at the bus stop to make sure I made it safely. By the time Adam had reached the age of eight, he had two younger half-brothers whom Abby also abused. It was not unusual to get a telephone call from Abby asking me to come and get Adam "before I kill him." I always did. In spite of questions and strange looks from my family, friends, and neighbors, Adam and I remained close. But Abby always wanted him back.

One morning, on my way to court, Abby called me on the telephone. She had a sad story. "Come and get him, Lillian," she sobbed. "Take him. You can get custody of him. They're trying to lock me up." I was ecstatic. I loved Adam with all my heart and now I could have him and I could save him. I could rescue him. He was only eight years old, and it could not possibly be too late, could it? Abby was waiting for an answer. "I'm sorry," I said. "Of course, I will take him." For my very best project of all, the timing was perfect. I was leaving town soon to take the bench in Fresno, California as a federal administrative law judge with the Social Security Administration. As his legal guardian, I could take him with me and he would be mine forever. Within a week, I enrolled Adam in the public school down the street and in the after-school program a block away.

But Adam's first week in the new school did not go well. The teachers complained that he was aggressive and starting fights. Adam claimed that he was defending himself from violent bullies. The second week was worse. Adam was disruptive and refused to sit still. None of the complaints bothered me. He was still the Adam that I had always loved and I knew that, in California, I would find an educational program tailored to his unique needs. The third week, Adam refused to go to school. I dressed him anyway, but I was unable to put shoes on him without his cooperation. Undaunted, I took him out of the house barefoot, carrying his shoes in my hand. It took him only one block of stones and broken glass to ask to put the shoes on. I was confident that I could handle any problem that Adam might present.

The very next morning, walking out of my bedroom, I smelled smoke. I ran to Adam's bedroom downstairs and saw him extinguishing flames in the middle of the floor. He had started a fire with a book of matches, bamboo sticks, several of my business cards—which he had shredded up—and silk fabric from a kite that had hung on the wall. A year before, Adam had started a fire in the same room and we had a long talk then about playing with matches. But this time was different. Adam scattered the ashes and gazed miserably at the six-inch-long burn mark on the grey wall-to-wall carpet. Then he began to cry and apologize. "Get dressed," I ordered him. "I'm going to be late for court." I gathered up the debris from the fire, made sure the ashes were cool, and shoved it into a plastic bag. I was too angry to talk, and I had no idea what to say. Was I too late for Adam?

When I finished my court appearance, I walked to the office of the social workers in the courthouse. I needed help. "I am the legal guardian of a child in the neglect system," I explained. "He tried to set my house on fire this morning." I showed them the debris in the plastic bag. "My house is not safe anymore. What should I do? This is the second time he has set a fire in my house." All the social workers agreed on the solution to my problem. "Take him to a shelter and leave him there," they said. I knew that was not the right answer. "Do you have an alternative to a shelter?" I asked. "That just seems really cold. He is only eight years old." Amused at my concern for an unrelated child who had committed a destructive act, they said, "Take him to any fire station. They will take care of him and make sure he is safe." That was not the solution I was looking for, either. "Something is wrong with him," I protested. "Isn't there somewhere I can take him to make sure he gets the help he needs?" The women were getting frustrated with me. "Well, you could try Saint Elizabeth's Mental Hospital. They have a section that specializes in disturbed children. Call this number for a psychiatrist appointment. There is a slight chance that they will decide to admit him there on the same day he's examined." They all thought I was a fool to care about the mental state of someone who tried to burn my house down, even if he was just a child .

Adam had spent so much time with me that he had become part of my family. My niece, who had come to live with me for several years, had met Adam as an infant when she was fourteen years old. Whenever she could, she would wrap him in a blanket and take him around her girlfriends in the neighborhood. If her peers questioned her about him she would announce proudly that he was her baby. As soon as Adam could eat solid food, she took him to fast-food restaurants and fed him burgers and fries without my permission. A happy baby who never cried, Adam turned into a curious toddler and a helpful child. My daughter, a gifted young artist, painted Adam's portrait as a young adult in a sailor uniform when he was only six years old. She never told me that Adam was the model for the young man and I did not make the connection until years later, when Adam spied the painting mounted on the wall in my house and recognized himself. Adam trusted me to watch out for him and to save him. How could I desert him now? My daughter had refused to relocate to California with me. I would not force her to leave her friends. Would I have to leave Adam behind too? I had no idea when I might return to the East Coast, and I had always wanted to live on the other side of the country.

As soon as I left the courthouse, I called the number. I told the psychiatrist what happened with the fires. "Where is the child?" she asked, unable to disguise a note of alarm on the last word. "He is in school, in class," I answered, wondering why she sounded so worried. "Take him out of the building immediately and bring him straight to my office," she demanded, making no attempt this time to hide the panic in her voice. "He might set fire to the school today."

The boy and I were soon waiting outside her office in a large brick building on the manicured hospital grounds. I was familiar with the complex, having visited Chee Chee and Tony, as well as several clients, there over the years. Adam played with the toys scattered in the area and chatted amiably with the armed guard. "I like your hat," Adam said. "Can I see your gun? I want to be a police like you when I grow up." The doctor met with me first. "He is becoming more sophisticated with his technique," she said after carefully examining the debris in the bag. The progression from mere matches a year ago to the paper, wood, and silk demonstrates that he is acquiring more skill. The next fire will be more successful." Her interview with Adam, behind the closed door, did not last long. She emerged with a frown on her face. "I have determined that Adam presents a danger to himself and to others," she said. "You must leave him here today. We will be in touch with you in reference to visiting arrangements. Adam has set fires in the mother's house as well as yours."

I was stunned. "I don't understand," I said, surprised to learn of fires on Robinson Place. "If he set fires at home, why didn't his mother tell me about them?" The psychiatrist shook her head from side to side, not shocked by my question and certain of her assessment. "When he set the fires at home, he was beaten severely as punishment, but he was never treated for the underlying causes of the behavior," she explained. "His beatings taught him not to set fires again at home, so he simply set them in other locations. Thus, the fires at your home instead. For children younger than ten, the underlying cause is nearly always sexual trauma. I'm sorry," she added. "We will provide him with everything he needs here. You may say goodbye to him now, if you wish."

As Adam played with a new pile of toys, I said goodbye to his back. He stayed in the children's residential section for several years and then he became a ward of the city. When he turned twenty-one, he "aged out of the system." As much as I love him, I was unable to rescue him.

# Scene Twenty

## Something for Everyone

I was filled with patriotism when the band played *Hail to the Chief* on June 7, 1985. The president of the United States, Ronald Reagan, and the first lady, Nancy, entered the room to thunderous applause. It was a White House state dinner and I was there as Clarence's guest. The president had no idea who Clarence was and showed no hint of recognition as we approached the receiving line to shake his hand. In fact, the president seemed puzzled and frequently looked around with a vacant, distracted expression, as if he were trying to recall exactly where he was. An aide whispered Clarence's name and his title, chairman of the Equal Employment Opportunity Commission, in the president's ear, and a demented smile remained pasted on his face as we shook his hand and scurried past him, but I did not care. All I cared about was that I was in the same room and breathing the same air with Arnold Schwarzenegger. I had been crazy about him since my ex-husband had begun subscribing to muscle magazines that included his photographs. Arnold was not only the cutest of all the body builders, but he was also the most muscular, the funniest, the smartest, and the most charming. The camera loved Arnold too.

Shortly after his arrival from Eastern Europe, all the muscle magazines ran pages of photographs of him as he worked out in gyms with well-known title holders. Arnold's muscles grew and he began to garner fitness and body-building titles himself. He visited prisons and starred in a documentary about the arcane world of fitness. In his interviews, he described his dream of becoming a movie star in his newly-adopted country, which he loved so much. By the time he had been invited to the White House, he had added several Hollywood movies to that first documentary. His dream was coming true.

Inching my way through the crowd, I knew that I had to let him know what a fan I was, and I knew that I had to touch him. Finally, I stood beside him. I squeezed his swollen, steroid-enhanced bicep and simpered, "I loved all your movies. Will another one be released soon?" He smiled down on me, revealing a huge gap between his two upper-front teeth—just like mine. "Ja," he said, bouncing his head twice. I became emboldened. "Will they give you more than ten lines to say in the next one?" I asked. Maintaining his sense of humor, he grinned. "Ja," he said. "Iss possible." Then he introduced me to his fragile, elderly mother. Arnold was still single and she was his date. I stayed by his elbow and held a long, one-sided conversation with his non-English speaking mother. I told her all about myself and about Clarence, and then I asked her questions to which she could nod and reply, "Ja." "Do you like Washington?" I asked her. "Are you enjoying yourself here?" "The White House is beautiful, isn't it?" "Is this your first visit to the United States?"

I was not aware of this practice but learned that it is state dinner protocol to seat people who arrive together at different tables. I knew that Clarence would be miserable at his dinner table without me, as he found it difficult to make small talk with strangers. Although Clarence had already been quite politically active on behalf of the Republican party, neither of us knew anyone in the room very well. For dinner, I was seated at a table with White House staff members and journalists, who gleefully talked about themselves and rebuffed my efforts to change the subject. I felt sorry for Arnold's mother, stuck at a table without her son, and most likely ignored by everyone.

At some point in the long evening, I was astonished to see President Reagan engaged in an animated conversation. I made my way to his side and squeezed his bicep, too. "Your tuxedo is quite beautiful," I simpered. "Is it dark blue?" He looked at me and replied, "Why, yes it is." Then he resumed the conversation I had interrupted. He also resumed staring at the chests of the four beautiful twenty-something blondes who wore strapless dresses and crowded around him. The topic of the animated conversation was horses. I turned from the president and met the steadfast gaze of the first lady, who stood motionless nearby. She had barricaded herself behind a wooden table so that nobody could touch her or get within two feet of her. Gaunt and frail, Nancy had glazed, bulging eyes that were prescription-drug shiny. Golf-ball sized pearls nestled against her heavily-veined neck. When I introduced myself and told her that her necklace was beautiful, she nodded and continued to stare over my left shoulder at her excited husband. After the awful meal, Arnold rewarded me for being polite to his mother. He seated her next to me for the entertainment, and he sat on her other side. I was in heaven as I breathed in every wisp of second-hand smoke from the swollen, foul, black cigar that he savored during the concert. As a souvenir, I stole a small crystal glass that was made in France.

When I thanked Clarence for inviting me to the state dinner, he was shocked. "I would have accepted more White House invitations," he said, "but I thought you had such a low opinion of the president that you would be offended." We had been to a couple of formal receptions at the White House, but this was the first (and only) state dinner that I attended. "Well, it's not just a Republican White House," I countered. "It's mine, too." Marines in dress uniform prevented me from exploring the premises beyond the miniature gas-station style lavatory down the hall.

Clarence left Senator Danforth's office when he was appointed to a position in the Department of Education. He soon began to travel all over the country to make speeches on behalf of Republican candidates and issues. Eventually, his speeches and interviews attracted the attention of the press, and some unflattering stories emerged about him, especially when he began to criticize his own sister for being on welfare.

Clarence fumed when the press criticized him. After one particularly lengthy tantrum, I asked him whether the article had accurately quoted what he had said about his sister. He stopped in mid-sentence and told me that I was the only person who had asked that question all day. He did not bother to answer my question, but that ended the ranting to which I had been subjected. During this period of time, I introduced Clarence to my world. When I took him to a Howard Law School Alumni function, he was horrified and outraged because my friends hugged and kissed me during the event, and because I had left his side several times to get a beverage or search out someone whom I had not seen in several years. When we left for the parking lot, he was in such a traumatized state that he could only mumble repeatedly, "You let them touch you. They touched you."

The staff in Senator Biden's office were intensely curious about Clarence, and they wanted to know why I had begun to date him after he came looking for me a few times. Specifically, they wanted to know why I found him attractive. "He looks like an African warrior to me," I told them. Though this genuinely puzzled them, I was serious. Clarence even had several vertical scars running a couple of inches down one cheek. They probably were inflicted by his mother's long fingernails when he was an infant. My mother took responsibility for a scar that I had on my cheek, and it was a miniature version of Clarence's but, to me, his looked like tribal scars. I loved to lick them when I had an orgasm. When I took Clarence around my family, he was charming and laughed out loud like a child. As he drank, joked, ate, and danced with them, he seemed to enjoy their company more than I did. Indeed, I came to realize that Clarence was a lonely, depressed person who hid seething anger behind a veneer of conventional behavior.

Of course, I was familiar with the duality of rage and sacrificial conformity, the secret of the success of most educated black men I knew. The difference between them and Clarence, however, was that they were not surrounded by white, condescending Republicans. When I accompanied

Clarence to his social events, white men routinely came up to him and told him how proud they were of him. Clarence gritted his teeth and smiled, and then thanked them. When he attended social events with me, Clarence was barraged with questions. My family asked about his family, and my friends—black and white—routinely asked how he liked his new job or his newly adopted city, Washington, D.C. They also wanted to know how we met. Eventually, however, Clarence got into heated political debates with a variety of my family and friends, and those debates never went well. Clarence ended up raising his voice and accusing them of being unfair.

My world also included sexual experiences that were new to Clarence. I left Capitol Hill to enter private practice as a defense attorney shortly after Clarence left to join the Reagan administration. After my divorce, I shared custody of my young daughter with her father, and I moved back into the house that my ex-husband and I had purchased in my eighth month of pregnancy. As part of the divorce, I had bought him out of the house and, when I walked back through the door after an absence of less than two years, the sight of the filthy, poorly-maintained interior thoroughly shocked me. "What has he *done* to the house?" I screamed before I even knew that I was talking. All my life, my major source of escape had been reading but, for my ex-husband, his escape was hard-core pornography, especially movies. His father, a United States Park Police officer, first exposed him to porn. My father-in-law's job included the confiscation of illegal pornography, which he took home for his own viewing pleasure. Walter, as a young boy, discovered his father's stash and, eventually, the father tolerated the intrusions. After Walter reached twenty-one, his father gave him material for his own personal collection. The first porn that I ever watched was a brand new reel-to-reel sixteen-millimeter film that we had selected together from a rack in a local porn shop. Walter had promised to complete the laborious task of threading the film through the spools while I was at work, and then we would watch the movie together when I got home. When I entered the darkened room and saw how easy it would have been to flick the switch and run the projector, I asked him whether he had watched the movie without me. He lied, and started the movie. I was so shocked and excited by the images on the screen that I was rendered speechless and my mouth popped open.

After a few minutes, I remembered that Walter was in the room with me. He had not uttered a sound since the movie started, so I turned to see his face. To my amazement, he was not watching the wall onto which the images were being projected on a white sheet. Instead, his gaze was fixated on me. "You started without me, didn't you?" I asked. Nevertheless, that first movie started us on the path of chasing first-run, hard-core porn from city to city, for years. Philadelphia and New York City were our favorite venues. We sat in small neighborhood theaters that had been converted into darkened, mysterious places where no popcorn or sodas were sold, where we were usually the only couple, and where single men sat five seats apart and groaned softly during the slow-motion ejaculation scenes that featured volcano-like eruptions, usually on the face or torso of a writhing female. When the Linda Lovelace comedy *Deep Throat* hit the screen the press popularized hard-core porn and, finally, Walter and I began to see more couples in the darkened rows of the small theaters we frequented.

By the time I met Clarence, I was satiated with pornographic films, photographs, and magazines to the point of boredom. By then, Walter had unwittingly opened another door for me. That door had its lock firmly in place, even while I was in law school. A fellow student there, Gerard, had become obsessed with me. Although I never encouraged his ardor, my refusals merely made him more persistent, and he was absolutely confident that he would one day melt my heart. When he told me that he had recently married a very beautiful and much younger woman with red hair and a curvaceous body, and that he would love for me to meet her, I was totally clueless. I could not imagine why he could think that such a development would make him more attractive to me. Eventually, this persistent suitor invited Walter and me on a boat trip with him and his bride. The boat trip sounded like fun, especially since about fifty other people would be sailing with us, and I was curious about the woman he married. I kept Walter ignorant of my friend's agenda and, ever anxious to please me, he agreed to the outing.

The wife turned out to be as beautiful as Gerard had described. Her hair was fragrantly, naturally red and fell in large waves down her bare back. She wore a strapless, tight denim mini dress that revealed huge mounds of breasts, a tiny waist, and a heart-shaped rear. Her thighs and calves were rounded and firm and, when she smiled and threw her head back to laugh, she looked like a movie star. Although she was freckled and very light-skinned, her broad lips, mouth, and generous nose made her easily identifiable as black. On the boat, she quickly took a fancy to my husband. This development amused me and I began to understand what was happening as the boat docked, when my clever, manipulative suitor suggested that both couples return to our nearby apartment.

Gerard first made sure that my husband and his seductive wife were comfortable in the bedroom, where they caressed and fondled each other as they stripped naked. Then, across the hall in the living room, Gerard and I began to dance slowly to Teddy Pendergrass. Somehow, my clothes got strewn all over the floor and I was looking at a twelve-inch long penis attached to a nude, scrawny gargoyle of a man. I had to have it. We were both writhing on the floor, moaning in ecstasy in competition with the music, half under the sofa, when his wife and my husband, both completely naked, walked out of the bedroom. Walter was sobbing. "My wife! My wife!" he said hysterically, as I grabbed for my clothes. Walter had not succumbed to the wife's charms and he was appalled at the sight of the two of us on the floor. Gerard's wife comforted Walter in the doorway.

"Don't worry," she said. "It will be okay. It's fine. You will be okay. You'll see."

It took all three of us to get him calmed down, although Gerard's efforts to touch my husband's shoulder or arm nearly precipitated a fist fight. But, a couple of hours later, we all ended up emotionally and physically exhausted in the same bed. The men were on the outside and the wife and I lay beside each other. I made sure I was not touching her as she slept, but as I lay half asleep myself, Gerard picked up my hand from the bed. He tenderly placed it on top of his wife's naked, carefully trimmed vagina and pushed my fingers inside the slippery heat. An electrical shock pulsed from my wet fingertips, through every fiber of my body, ending in an explosion somewhere in my brain. She moaned. A fire was lit, and a door blasted open. This was my first physical sexual contact with another woman, but it would not be my last.

My husband, Gerard's wife, and I developed a close sexual and emotional relationship that I considered to be ideal. Eventually, like all good things, the trio deteriorated, but it was soon replaced with another one. A proud, Jewish attorney, Rita was young and unmarried, with lush hennaed hair down to her nineteen-inch waist. I introduced her to my husband.

My first sexual encounter with her occurred in the bed with him. Walter woke from a sound sleep to find Rita's face buried in my crotch, while she groaned loudly enough to wake up the neighbors on the other side of the bedroom wall. A few minutes earlier, she had left the living room sofa, where she was supposed to spend the night, and crept into our bedroom. It was her first sexual relationship with a woman. Rita was even more beautiful than our first partner and we all fell in love with each other. Every kiss, caress, and touch of these women seemed miraculous to me, and I treasured the experiences and the time that they so generously gave me. Although I tried to reciprocate, I always felt that I received much more from them than I gave. I wondered whether men felt that same lack of balance about the women in their lives.

When Clarence entered my world, it had been years since I had been in a conventional relationship. For me, Clarence was a national treasure, to be enjoyed to the fullest extent possible and certainly to be shared. He already had a strong interest in pornography. A small video shop near Dupont Circle had become familiar with his preferences and they let him know when material arrived that might interest him. Although I had little interest in the genre, I never discouraged his forays and I pretended to enjoy what excited him. Huge breasts on naked obese women and slow-motion male ejaculations from long penises were his preferences. Both bored me.

Clarence, on the other hand, was easily entertained and aroused. Whenever I could, I hired magicians to perform at parties and Clarence laughed and smiled like a child at every stupid card trick, disappearing coin, and tossed ring. I took him to visit my family and he danced and told jokes until three in the morning. Finally, I took him to Plato's Retreat, a private club that occupied a long warehouse block in Manhattan. Plato's Retreat was open to the public for a fee, and it was there that I discovered that Clarence liked to watch. The club had something for everyone. For those who liked to fondle and engage in sex acts with strangers, the big room was clothing optional. Reclining on couches and rugs, couples and singles allowed strangers to touch them and watch them. It was mostly a big grope session but, while we relaxed there, Clarence frowned and swatted away fingers and hands if a male touched him or me anywhere on our bodies. No liquor was served or allowed on the premises, but there was a buffet for the hungry and juice for the thirsty. For those who liked to dance, a huge dance floor with rock music always attracted scantily dressed members who gyrated and caressed. Clarence did not dance much there, but he greedily watched others from the edge of the wooden floor. For water lovers, there was an indoor heated swimming pool with skinny dipping. Clarence sometimes entered the pool, but his very favorite amenity was a set of small, private rooms for those who liked to watch. These rooms had windows set at eye level for those who liked to peep into the room, and the door could be pulled shut though it could not be locked from the inside or the outside. Wooden benches were bolted into the floor and walls.

Inside the walls of these rooms, sadists often wielded whips, studded gloves, and bare hands to induce grunts and moans from kneeling, willing masochistic victims in an almost intoxicating mixture of pleasure and pain. As Clarence scampered from one room to another, the skimpy white club-issued towel around his waist became a tent that could not hide his enormous erection. My reward from him for an evening at Plato's Retreat was passionate, intense, utterly silent intercourse with him in creative positions in one of the private rooms. A steady parade of patrons entered and exited the small room behind Clarence's perspiring back for several hours until the club closed at dawn.

Clarence did not like his body and his hair was a constant source of frustration for him. When his hair was soaking wet, he used a black plastic comb with needle-sized teeth for grooming, and he grunted as he ripped the circular strands from their roots in an effort to control the beady curls. As a result of this self-destruction, he had to brush profuse sprinkles of loose hairs from his back and shoulders each morning before dressing. His face was also a source of angst. To prevent acne, Clarence had to tweeze facial hairs constantly. Blood spurted from his skin as the tweezers grabbed and then yanked at the short hairs that insisted on curling back to the skin and burrowing beneath it, causing an infection at the site of each of the sparse hairs on his face. Years of weightlifting had failed to eliminate his pot belly, which emerged at the edge of his chest and protruded below his navel, and Clarence ran miles each day to prevent weight gain. His legs were disfigured by ropy protrusions of varicose veins, which he eventually eliminated by surgery. Clarence's feet were wide and flat, but his toes were deformed at a forty-five-degree angle by years of cheap shoes that were worn too small. Clarence is bowlegged and pigeon-toed; these characteristics made him a great runner, but they also forced him to adopt a shambling gait, and he appears to be dragging his feet when he walks.

Clarence never thought he was good-looking, but I told him he was beautiful and I believed him when he said that I was the first woman to tell him that. His almond-shaped eyes slant upward at the edges to give the upper third of his face an Asian quality. His nostrils start out flat at the bridge of his nose and then flare out dramatically to open wide on each side, like a lily. His very high and sharp cheekbones jutted out above a jaw that was fully defined and nearly always clenched in anger. His lips are dramatic. They start out flat at the fully defined demarcation line with his skin, with a rim that sets them apart. This flatness gives way to a gradual roundness and puffiness, like a balloon as it gets inflated. His lips blossom in a perpetual kiss. Even when he is angry, Clarence cannot force his lips to disappear. His mouth sits there and demands attention of some sort. Clarence's skin has no visible pores, and it is so smooth that it has the appearance of a liquid rather than a solid. He touched me like an exploring child would, or a blind person, and when he gets excited, he sighs like a woman.

Clarence and I traveled together. His drunken ruminations about his miserable childhood and his mistreatment at the hands of adults generated fits of anger, resentment, and self-pity that left him exhausted. Clarence's grandfather was the main focus of his complaints. I thought that a trip to Savannah and Pinpoint, Georgia might serve to exorcise the demons by allowing his rants to be placed in context. My imagination, fueled by Clarence's anger, had created a fetid swamp, slums, shacks, outhouses, kerosene lamps, and abject poverty. But Clarence parked the rental car, and we walked through a clearing toward the jetty, where the crab-processing warehouse used to stand. "My mother used to work here," Clarence explained. She was a kind of factory crab-picker. At the edge of the clearing, an ocean of swaying, shoulder-high tan-green grasses came into view, as far as the eye could see, all the way to the horizon. Once upon a time, crabs thrived at the base of the grasses, and flat boats made paths through the water to snare them for sale. Although the crabs had been destroyed, the vegetation that had sheltered them remained. As I stared at the undulating stalks, I whispered, "This is the most beautiful sunset I have ever seen, Clarence." He had grown up beside an ocean of grass that responded to the slightest breeze with murmurs and waves that could be duplicated nowhere else.

Clarence turned quickly from the stunning landscape, and we crossed a dirt road to the nearby wooden home of his sister. Covered with peeling paint, it was surrounded by mobile homes and trailers of white people who used the area as their second home. Many children and adults were inside the house, which was dark and crowded with Clarence's nieces, nephews, and cousins. I was unable to determine who the occupants were, but they were all happy to see Clarence. When I introduced myself, they all seemed shy and withdrawn. We also visited Clarence's mother's home, where she and her boyfriend graciously cooked dinner for us and made sure we were comfortable.

The high point of the trip for me was the excursion to the bar, a double-wide trailer where the local moonshine was sold by the glass. After drinking two ounces—to the amusement of the customers crowded in the trailer's kitchen—I took a mason jar of this clear, powerful corn liquor home with me. Most of our time in Georgia we spent in Savannah, where Clarence pointed out schools he had attended and other sites of significance in his childhood. He and his brother had been taken in by his grandfather, a nearly illiterate, self-employed man who was gruff, cruel, and physically and emotionally abusive. He had delivered fuel oil and performed other chores in the area for fees that he collected from businesses and homeowners. A highly religious Catholic, the grandfather's fondest wish was that Clarence would become a priest. When Clarence quit the seminary, as a result of the cruel pranks and gross racism to which he was subjected on a daily basis, the grandfather upbraided him and viewed the harassment as no excuse for abandonment of the priesthood.

The grandfather himself had belittled Clarence for years, accusing him of being lazy, ugly, sleeping too much, and never working hard enough to ensure that Clarence did not meet the fate of his peers and the peers of his grandfather. According to the grandfather, these men, were "no-good niggers who would never amount to anything and were always looking for a handout from white people." In his world, white people were the heroes, and they were to be feared, imitated, and respected—not blamed. Racism and the history of slavery in the United States did not exist as reasons for economic deprivation. Rather, in his worldview, moral depravity was the cause of failure and laziness was the greatest sin. The grandfather prided himself on his own ability to work long into the night without resting or sleeping, to endure pain, and to overcome hunger and cold. Clarence's childhood never furnished enough rest, food, or comfort to make it a tolerable existence.

Clarence's decision to enter the seminary was the grandfather's only source of pride in Clarence, and he used that status to brag to the neighborhood about what he had done for Clarence and his brother. Thus, Clarence's departure from the seminary caused an estrangement from his grandfather that was never repaired. Clarence refused to visit him when the man grew ill, and I spent hours persuading him to at least attend the funeral, which he did without me. During these discussions, I learned that the grandfather had a tender relationship with Clarence's ex-wife and young son, who had visited him several times and talked with him by telephone. Like many abused children, Clarence was ambivalent toward his mother and grandfather, wanting to please them but also hating them for the pain and disappointment they had caused him when he needed them the most. I understood Clarence only because of my own miserable childhood.

During the several days that we spent in Pinpoint and Savannah, Georgia, we went to the theatre, saw movies, and ate some great restaurant meals. His constant uniform in both areas consisted of a torn, dark-blue Yale Law School tee shirt with the school's name in eight-inch block letters stenciled across his chest. He called every white man "Sir" and smiled at them. He did not look any white woman in the face and he did not speak directly to any white woman. When I asked him to stop doing that, he looked confused. He was unable to stop.

Our best trips were probably the ones to the Caribbean. After we checked in, he slept about forty hours straight, skipping meals and waking only for short bouts of sex. He was obviously sleep-deprived.

Clarence was a great prankster. My first and only parasailing experience occurred when Clarence said it looked like a lot of fun. He promised me that he would get strapped into the parachute and get pulled off the pier by the tiny speedboat if I did it first. This would be a small price to pay to ensure that Clarence had a good time, so I agreed. Swallowing my great fear of heights, I cursed and screamed at the top of my lungs, starting within the first six feet of my ascent from the beach. The pilot of the boat must have heard me, as he staged dramatic dips to the water, causing my toes to trail in the surf as the sunbathers grinned and then waved at my rapidly climbing form. Though extended for the entertainment of the pilot, the ride probably lasted no longer than half an hour, but it seemed an eternity before my toes touched down on the floating pier. I yanked off the straps and turned to assist Clarence into the parachute. He exploded in laughter. He shouted, "I would never do anything that stupid and dangerous!" And he never did.

Clarence's relationships with his ex-wife and his son Jamal were sources of great frustration for him. When Jamal was living with his mother, Clarence had long, heated telephone conversations with his ex-wife about the child in my apartment. Unable to cope with Jamal, the mother regularly asked Clarence for his advice and assistance. As I sat silently in my living room, Clarence ranted and raved about her inability, invariably ending the conversation with the admonition that it was her responsibility to care for her child and to raise him properly. The pregnancy had been unplanned, and Clarence blamed her for bringing his son into the world without his permission.

Eventually, Clarence was persuaded to have his son reside with him in a large apartment in Maryland, but he was not happy about the new arrangement. The telephone rants to the mother were replaced with diatribes directed to the child himself. Jamal was excoriated at great length for every dereliction, from failure to clean his bedroom and bathroom to the loss of his prescription eyeglasses. Although Jamal maintained that he mislaid the glasses, I always assumed that he lost them in fights with bullies or had them snatched from his face by older classmates. The missing eyeglasses were a constant source of irritation for Clarence, particularly because Jamal could not complete his prodigious amounts of homework assignments at the private school without the eyeglasses, nor could he see the blackboard without them. Each missing pair, therefore, had to be replaced as soon as possible. As a result of the verbal abuse that followed the confession of loss, Jamal waited as long as possible before sharing the bad news of subsequent incidents. Each time Jamal informed his father of the loss of a new pair of glasses, his description of the disappearance became more fantastic, and Clarence became increasingly agitated and abusive as Jamal fell further behind in his schoolwork.

The move to the Maryland apartment strained Clarence's finances. I had refused his request to move into the townhouse that I had acquired in the divorce, and I never told Clarence that my precocious, highly verbal daughter did not particularly like the older, shy, withdrawn Jamal or that she told me that our house would be "too crowded" with the addition of Clarence and his son, even if they had their own bedroom. Soon, Clarence began throwing tantrums whenever Jamal asked for money for school fees or whenever it became obvious that the growing boy needed to replace his shoes or clothes. This verbal abuse reminded me too much of my own painful childhood, but Clarence was out of control. I loaned him two-thousand dollars when he asked for it, but it really did not help the situation.

Although Clarence was fastidious and almost obsessively clean about his person and clothing, his clothing reflected his dire financial straits. His shirts and ties were frayed and all of his suits were shiny from constant wear. He owned only one pair of dress shoes, which he repaired constantly. His underwear and socks were in tatters. Clarence reluctantly cooked for himself and his son. His specialty was lasagna, which he prepared with the attention to detail and total focus that he brought to all the important tasks of his life. I learned to sit primly and silently on the kitchen counter and watch or read a book while he performed this fatherly ritual. It was impossible to tell whether he detested his kitchen duties or whether these habitual tasks gave him some sense of comfort and peace. In either case, offers of assistance in the kitchen were spurned or cruelly criticized for their incompetence in execution. It made no difference whether the offers came from me or from Jamal.

When I visited Niagara Falls in Canada, I heard that the entire scenic area had been purchased by one man, who promptly erected a huge fence around the perimeter and charged a fee to allow visitors to gaze at the rapids through a hole that had been carved in the wooden fence.

Eventually, the Canadian government purchased the land from him and opened it to the public, who can now view it fenceless and without charge. I guess it made me like the Canadian government but, to me, Clarence was like the Grand Canyon or a sunset or a huge waterfall—a force of nature to be enjoyed. Early in my sexual relationship with Clarence, I had decided that he should be shared with other women. Not sharing him would have been just wrong.

Our first partner was a woman whom I had already shared with an ex-lover. Light-skinned, tall, and physically beautiful, she was neurotic, emotionally passive, and perfect for Clarence. She sucked toes, vaginal lips, and large penises with equal relish, and was the best kisser on the planet. Unfortunately, with his stocky build, dark skin, and lack of sophistication, Clarence was the opposite of every lover she had experienced, but she was willing to try it. Our encounters as a threesome were of epic proportions. Like all of the lovers I have known with long and thick shafts, it was impossible for Clarence to find a condom that would comfortably fit, so these sessions were not marred by that bit of awkwardness and Clarence's joy knew no bounds as he was caressed and licked and sucked over every inch of his body by two women with oral fixations. He could not fake the moans or the many ejaculations, and his erection rarely flagged for very long. Both of us probably fell in love with her but, for me, it is difficult to distinguish between love and lust.

One of Clarence's most painful memories was of a white woman who lived on or near some property that he maintained as an adolescent. An important part of his grandfather's business was doing yard work for rich whites who owned large estates around Savannah. One of these estates had an enormous outdoor swimming pool and the blonde lady of the house routinely sunbathed in the nude as she watched Clarence perform garden chores. The humiliation of performing manual labor while a pampered white woman intentionally teased him with her forbidden flesh fueled a burning resentment that Clarence clung to and described with drunken tears of anguish. As he matured physically, women verbally or unconsciously told him that he was ugly. At Holy Cross, he met a brown-skinned townie who had come on campus for a date with Clarence's smooth-talking, handsome classmate. The classmate stood her up for a better offer and Clarence seized the opportunity. He married her because "she was the first woman who was nice" to him. She got pregnant immediately. Clarence was devastated because he never wanted children but, after a spate of arguments about the subject, the unwanted pregnancy fortunately ended in a "miscarriage." A second unplanned pregnancy resulted in Jamal's birth before Clarence's graduation from law school. Realizing that he could not trust the birth-control issue to his wife, Clarence got a vasectomy. Problem solved. I found the slightly keloid scar and licked it whenever I could.

After Clarence's legal career was established in Missouri, women began to approach him and aggressively flirt with him. He was always suspicious of their motives. These were the same kind of women who had found him unattractive in the past and who had been so unkind to him. When he joined a co-ed gym, women sometimes asked him if they could touch his glistening, hairless chest. When I asked him how he responded to this harmless flirtation ritual, he snorted sarcastically. "I always told them they could touch my chest," he bragged, "if they let me touch theirs first!" Sadly, they never did.

Of course, I was happy to secure for Clarence his first white sex partner. I had the perfect candidate. She was a tall redhead, with green eyes, a sunny disposition, and a beautifully slender body and face. Although she had never experienced a black male sex partner, she was willing to succumb to her curiosity. When I introduced them, they both seemed comfortable; Clarence was his charming self and she genuinely liked him, so the sexual encounter was planned for late evening a few days later. Everybody appeared and clothes were shed. But, for the first time since I had known him, Clarence was unable to perform sexually. Efforts by the two of us to get him relaxed, to comfort him, or to ignore him all failed. The poor man was so embarrassed and miserable that she got dressed and drove herself home. Distraught after her departure, Clarence explained that the experience with the sunbather and the Southern rule that white women were forbidden as objects of desire had terrified him more than he ever wanted to admit.

I became even more determined to get the arrangement consummated. Clarence could not be allowed to continue living with this kind of impediment. Clarence spent more time with her outside the bedroom and learned that she was a legal secretary who had grown up in Georgia and had worked near Capitol Hill. In spite of the racial difference, they discovered that they had a lot in common. They quickly became friends and, finally, everyone agreed to give it one more try. In the bedroom the second time around, she treated him with love and empathy, and Clarence performed like the phenomenon he truly was. She eventually asked whether all black men were built like Clarence. "Of course they are!" I said. "Haven't you heard?"

I suppose it was to be expected that Clarence would want to contribute to our sexual menu. His first addition was a high-strung, very intense, slender dark-skinned woman whom I met in the bedroom. Clarence ordered her around like an animal and treated her with disdain. She silently removed her clothes when he told her to and she obeyed his commands with alacrity, but it was soon clear that she was capable of performing only one sexual act with real enthusiasm. That act was masturbation while she observed one or both of us. I could not tell whether she was actually bringing herself to orgasm as she moaned and stroked herself frantically. Women can be very deceptive in the orgasm department, and I have often concluded that some women might not even know themselves whether they have climaxed or not. Clarence became increasingly angered by the woman's preoccupation, and he ordered her to stop and get dressed. She quickly put her clothes on and he drove her home. I never saw her again.

Clarence was not to be deterred. His second partner for a triangle refused to meet at my house, he said. Instead, it was arranged that I would meet the two of them at her house. When I arrived, the two of them were already in her bed and they appeared to have just finished a sex act. He had started without me, and I was not happy. At the foot of the bed was a television set with a porn movie still running. I had arrived about a half-hour late, straight from court, and Clarence was furious, but he tried to hide it. We eventually all got relaxed and enjoyed an exciting encounter that first-time, three-way sexual partnerships usually fuel. However, future encounters with this light-skinned, curvaceous partner, whom Clarence had described as "a pixie," were a little different. Like Clarence, she was obsessed with porn. Ideally, all sexual activity for her occurred while she was watching a movie at the foot of her bed. Like the masturbator, she was passive and almost worshipful of Clarence. She told me that the only reason she had agreed to a threesome was that she was curious about his other sex partners. It never occurred to me that Clarence might be monogamous, but it was obvious that jealousy was a motivating factor for her. Eventually, she revealed that she was very upset when she saw me for the first time because I was not ugly. So, when I walked into the bedroom that first time, Clarence was angry that I was late, I was disappointed that they had started without me, and she was jealous of the other woman. Isn't sex grand?

While we were in the relationship, Clarence was appointed Chairman of the Equal Employment Opportunity Commission (EEOC). We had a running joke about his new office space. After he was first shown the space, he attempted to describe it to me, but I was confused because he seemed to simultaneously disparage it and brag about it. I finally gave up and just asked him outright what he thought about his new office. He frowned. "It is much too large," he said with a dismissive shake of his head. This sentence was so demonstrative of his inability to enjoy life and to appreciate what was offered to him and of his need to shun what gave him pleasure and to hide his true character that I burst out laughing. He had to laugh too. "It is much too large" became our personal code for what he failed to appreciate and for his false protestations of modesty and humility. A very ambitious, angry man, Clarence wore a mask, and he knew it. As time passed, he gave new speeches and formed new friendships, and his mask became firmly affixed until it could never be removed again. The cynical mask eventually replaced his sexual preferences, his spontaneity, his sense of humor, and his humanity.

On the day of his swearing-in ceremony, I was running late from court, as usual. I was still about five blocks from the EEOC building when I was flagged down by a man riding a motorcycle. It was Clarence's best friend, Gilbert Hardy, another attorney. They had attended law school together. In many ways, Gilbert was Clarence's opposite—thin, genuinely friendly, a diver, snow skier, and a charmer. Before his death in a scuba accident, I represented him in an amicable divorce from his young wife. Gil and I arrived on the motorcycle together, to catch the last few minutes of the ceremony, but we both pretended we had been there from the start. One of Clarence's white nun-teachers from his Catholic grade school was there, smiling broadly at everyone. I could not figure out why she was there, since everything Clarence had tearfully told me about those years featured nuns who punished him physically and verbally for having kinky hair, ragged clothes, and other characteristics over which he had no control. Neither his grandfather nor any other adult in Clarence's life had any connection to the nuns and priests who made his early educational experiences a nightmare. It took me a while to realize that the nun, like his new religiosity, was a bow to the born-again Christian right.

At EEOC, I met Anita Hill and other members of Clarence's staff for the first time. Clarence complained incessantly about her, describing each professional confrontation he had with her in great detail. He insisted that I visit his office and wait there for his driver as often as I could, but I hated going to his office. The atmosphere was very tense and the employees were usually rude to each other and to me, but they were rather simpering in the presence of Clarence. Nevertheless, I humored him and visited the EEOC as often as I could. When I finally asked Clarence what the problem was between him and Anita Hill, he explained that she was jealous and wanted the same relationship with him and access to him that she'd had at the Department of Education. Though she had followed him to the EEOC, her initial connection with Clarence had been through Gil Hardy. Clarence finally solved the Anita Hill problem by getting her a teaching job outside the city. Of course, some problems just get worse, and a mere relocation did not solve this problem. When the problem surfaced at the confirmation hearing, Clarence told me that it would never have happened if Gil had still been alive. Thus, Gil's death was a double blow for Clarence. His best friend had died, and Clarence had no leverage over Anita Hill. Left to his own devices, Clarence was unable to fathom why she had accused him. "Why did she do it?" he asked repeatedly. "Why did she do it?" He was dumbfounded. I had no answer.

As Clarence became more involved in Bush Senior's presidential campaign, he began to unravel. His bitterness and resentment surrounding his abusive childhood and his abandonment by his mother and father devolved into punitive polemics aimed at his sister, who had given birth to several children without marrying. She lived in poverty. He weaved his assertions into highly-publicized speeches that made him the darling of Republicans nationwide.

Meanwhile, his health became a source of great anxiety for Clarence. For months, he thought he was going blind, but he never mentioned it to me until an eye doctor finally diagnosed the problem.

Though he thought he was developing blind spots, which he could identify by staring at a white wall, they were merely floaters, harmless bits of cellular debris that travel regularly over the eyeball. Some people, like Clarence, just have more of them.

Clarence also gradually developed a refusal to sleep normally, and mentioned his ability to function on very little sleep in interviews and speeches. On some important level, however, he must have known that his grandfather, who bragged about subsisting on a mere three hours of sleep each night, napped during the day while Clarence and his brother were at school or performing some back-breaking chore in the fields. But Clarence's efforts to emulate the man he professed to despise resulted in sleep deprivation so severe that, for several weeks, he thought he was dying. Again, he never mentioned these fears to me until a doctor correctly diagnosed his physical symptoms as mere sleep deprivation.

Clarence's travel and speech obligations on behalf of the Republican Party grew and eventually took their toll on him mentally and physically. He became obsessed with the bunched veins in his calves and underwent elective surgery to remove what he regarded as grotesque disfigurements of his legs. I could barely see what he found so disgusting, because the color of his skin perfectly hid the condition. While he was in the hospital recuperating from the surgery, I attended a Prince concert. After court on the evening of the show, I squeezed in a trip to his hospital room, though I had to curtail the visit. Incensed that I would attend a rock concert while he was hospitalized, Clarence told me after his discharge that it would be very difficult for him to forgive such hurtful behavior.

Clarence did not allow any displays of physical, romantic, sexual, or emotional feelings around his son Jamal, with the exception of Clarence's own verbal abuse of the boy. Eventually, Clarence's irritability escalated to the point where he regularly turned his back to me as he slept in our shared bed, and he pretended not to notice my coded sexual advances, such as a leg thrown over his. This behavior coincided with his increasing religiosity. He began rising a half-hour earlier each morning so that his driver could stop by a Catholic Church and wait for Clarence to visit inside before proceeding to the EEOC. Still, he was the first to arrive for the workday, as he made sure to mention in his speeches and interviews. He also  mentioned his church visits in an interview shortly after their commencement.

Clarence inexorably eliminated every aspect of his life that gave him joy.  We no longer traveled together or attended movies, plays, or concerts. We no longer pursued threesomes, and Clarence seldom visited my house. Although I stayed overnight at the new apartment he shared with his son, I was limited to three nights a week and he ignored me for much of that time, as Clarence coped with his cooking and parental duties and his EEOC work schedule, as well as a highly controlled  Republican campaign. The press interviews, which he seldom refused, were often conducted by telephone at home and frequently kept him talking until well after midnight during the week. Clarence  even stopped drinking alcohol, without  rehabilitation or counseling, and when others imbibed in his presence he ordered  non-alcoholic beer. His morning and weekend running became self-punishing  rituals that required ever longer recovery periods. I wondered whether I was the only one who had concluded that he had been an alcoholic for  many  years.

Though my family and friends had found him funny and charming when they first met him, Clarence eventually alienated all of them. His public speeches and interviews were mystifying to them, and I was unable to defend him. How could I explain that Clarence had a lot to prove, that he despised poor people who were his own color, and that criticism of him by black intellectuals enraged him and drove him to vow vengeance? How could I tell them that he eagerly adopted and regularly muttered to himself one of his very favorite quotes from his grandfather: "Niggers and flies,

I do despise. The more I see Niggers, the more I like flies."? They would not have believed me.

Clarence was convinced that Bush Senior really liked him. When I accompanied Clarence to the White House, President Reagan could not recall Clarence's name or title, but Vice President Bush developed a different relationship with the man who campaigned so diligently for him, who befriended Rush Limbaugh, and who gave speeches, on short notice, before small groups of born-again Christians and moderate Republicans all over the South and West. Clarence was eventually rewarded by appointments to the Federal Court of Appeals for the District of Columbia Circuit and to the Supreme Court, but I had left him before his first appointment to the bench. He told me later that a source of great resentment for him was my habit of reading. Clarence hated the fact that he could not read books for pleasure.

# Scene Twenty-One
## Adorable in a Bathing Suit

The voice on the telephone was the perfect combination of sexy and professional, a blend of Bette Davis and Marilyn Monroe. It belonged to Barbara, the Biden staffer who handled personnel matters that would bring me from the United States Attorney's Office in the District of Columbia to the United States Senate. The timing was perfect for my departure from the Civil Division. Although I had been in the assignment for less than a year, I had whittled down my caseload from several dozen to fewer than six. In the process of doing that, due to my strange ability to grasp arcane accounting principles and reduce them to simple patterns, I had acquired some expertise in the area of disappointed bidders. As the newest attorney in the Division, I had been assigned to emergency applications for temporary restraining orders, which required comprehension of contracting issues and government-procurement rules. My ability to speed read and comprehend voluminous data enabled me to dispose of these complex matters with ease. Finally, I was able to clear the cases without delays simply by providing false, early deadlines to the agency attorneys who were responsible for providing me with a first draft of court papers to be filed.

The problem with the Civil Division was that the case assignment system was due for computer monitoring very shortly. When that happened, it would become obvious to everyone that I had hardly any work pending on my calendar, and then I would be loaded down with new cases. Since the new cases would probably resemble the old cases that I had disposed of, little challenge lay ahead. On the other hand, I had been recruited to specialize in criminal forfeiture and to organize hearings on the issue for United States Senator Joseph Biden. This would be an exciting challenge, and I was looking forward to it. I was also looking forward to meeting Barbara in person. Without fully realizing it, my half-dozen telephone conversations with this complex voice had created a five-foot-seven, one-hundred-twenty-pound, dark-haired vixen with deep-set eyes and a firm handshake. After several weeks of bureaucratic red tape, I arrived at Barbara's office to meet her in the flesh. She climbed down from her chair, waddled toward me in a silky dress, and gave me a firm handshake as she introduced herself.

Unfortunately, I did not hear another word after Barbara said her name and shook my hand. Drowning out every syllable she uttered, my brain was busy shouting her down, and it shouted the same sentence over and over for what seemed like an hour. "You are a midget! You are a midget!" Yes, she was—with a pug nose, smashed-in face, stubby fingers, and bow legs. Her best features were her voice, milky, flawless skin, thick red, short-cropped hair, and wonderfully soulful big brown eyes. As the supervisor of unpaid interns, Barbara was a patient boss. As the human resources person in the general office, Barbara was a loyal Biden fan and a stickler for details. I admired her refusal to admit that she was different, even though tourists' children pointed at her and laughed in her face while their parents failed to admonish them, and even though strangers routinely insisted that she had to be "the one" who attended high school with them or lived in their neighborhood years ago. Long wooden stilt-like blocks were nailed to her car pedals so that she could drive her tiny car. Parking-lot attendants used their hands to manipulate her accelerator and brakes.

When we ate meals together, her stubby little fingers and lack of manual dexterity caused her to spill food all over her face and clothing. She just wiped most of it off and kept chattering away happily. When we walked down the street, I had to slow my speedy walk to a crawl so that her tiny legs could keep up, and so that she would not pant for breath. And when we went out to dance, I always insisted that prospective partners dance with her first. She loved music and she loved to dance. But, most of all, Barbara loved her job, which turned out to be in jeopardy after I had been in the office a couple of years.

I discovered that Barbara's job was in jeopardy by chance. Because she worked closely with the interns, Barbara's office was located in the basement, the floor below mine. Like most senators, Biden organized his staff at desks separated partially by tall partitions. While seated at my desk, I overheard senior administrative staff discussing Barbara. They concluded that she had to be fired. Tourists and constituents were drawn to Biden for several reasons. His youth, energy, friendliness, and exposure pursuant to his Judiciary Committee duties made him one of the most popular figures on the Hill. But Barbara's physical appearance, as she seized every opportunity to walk close to her god, Biden, had become an embarrassment. She would be fired as soon as they could find her replacement.

I knew that it would be really easy to replace Barbara. Young professionals with a master's degree in anything resembling political science always wanted to work for a popular senator like Biden. The competition would be fierce. I had to act soon. The next time I saw Clarence, I told him that, if he did not hire Barbara with a matching salary to do something in his office, I would never speak to him again. I knew that, as Chairman of the EEOC, he could do it and, although I was smiling when I made the threat, he could probably tell that I was serious. Since he had never met Barbara, I arranged for the two of them to be in the same place at the same time as soon as possible. As luck would have it, the next available time was a pool party at a friend's house in Northwest D.C. Since this was supposed to be a chance meeting, I could not warn Barbara that she would be meeting her future boss. I wanted her to act naturally because, when Barbara was nervous, she had a tendency to snort and giggle loudly.

When Clarence and I showed up at the pool party, I had already tried to prepare him for Barbara's appearance, but I was not prepared myself. She was sitting on the edge of the pool wearing a skimpy, two-piece bathing suit that revealed the deep arch of her back, which curved her entire torso into a C-shaped form. It failed to hide the beach-ball shaped hips that swelled from a twenty-inch waist and then abruptly gave way to grotesquely voluptuous thighs and calves. Bare for all the world to see, her tiny feet and stubby toes looked like they had been bound from birth. I was rendered speechless, but Clarence rushed toward her to shake the miniature hand. "Hi there," he gushed with a fake smile pasted on his face. "My name is Clarence. It's great to meet you. What's your name?"

It took all my persuasive powers to convince Barbara to abandon Biden and take the better-paying, secure, and challenging job opportunity that Clarence offered her. She cried like a baby at the big party we arranged for her departure, and Biden and the senior staff, posing with her for photographs, must have been marveling at their good fortune. Barbara and I were such good friends that I insisted she party at Tracks nightclub with me. The gay crowd, the trendy house music, the crowded dance floors, and the dancers were the best and biggest in the city in the early eighties. I had become obsessed with dancing there as often as I could and I left sweat-soaked and exhausted after three AM about twice a week. When Barbara told me she was in love and that she wanted me to meet the object of her affections, I knew where the encounter should be. Clarence had adamantly refused to set foot in Tracks because he was homophobic. Although he enjoyed watching and being watched at Plato's Retreat, the blatant homosexuality at Tracks was repugnant to him. Also I had never seen Clarence dance in public, so he would have been doubly uncomfortable at Tracks.

Barbara's boyfriend turned out to be an ultra-conservative midget who hated Tracks, left as soon as possible, and never spoke to me again. Because Barbara loved him, I advised her to go ahead and marry him if he proposed to her, but change the subject when he talked politics. After their wedding, I saw little of Barbara. I stopped calling her when she told me that she felt compelled to lie to her husband whenever we met for drinks or dinner. Barbara called me when she was tempted to quit her job at EEOC to take a private-sector job in human resources. Although the offers were always for a lower salary, she wondered whether she should seek greater challenges as her career blossomed under Clarence's benign but secret protection. She always followed my advice and stayed.

Several years ago, I heard that Barbara had died. At her memorial service, I offered my sympathy to the widower, and reminded him of who I was. He shook my hand coldly, told me he remembered me, and quickly turned to someone else. As I walked out of the chapel, I was fuming. Why had he not thanked me for keeping Barbara employed and getting her the job she loved? It took me a while to figure out the answer. I never told Barbara that she was getting fired from her Senate job, and I never told her that I forced Clarence to hire her. She died thinking that senior staff were devastated when she left Biden and that Clarence had hired her because she looked adorable in a bathing suit.

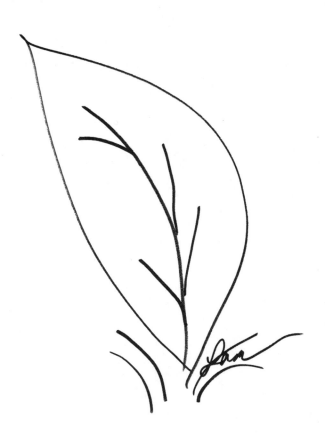

# Scene Twenty-Two
## Cheating Death

We were the last three passengers to board the bus that would discharge us two hours later at the Rio Grande Gorge. One of my fellow professors at the University of the District of Columbia Law School had persuaded me to join him and his partner for a full day of white-water rafting. We had all attended a professional conference in Albuquerque, New Mexico, spent the preceding day with his parents in the city, and then driven to Taos to board the bus. Although Mario and his partner had enjoyed the sport several times on western rivers, this would be my first time. Mario had convinced me that it would be fun but a little strenuous. Because I had no fear of the water, I was looking forward to it. Silly me.

I had never been afraid of any body of water. In fact, I had fallen in love with boating and all things related when I was fourteen years old. That was the year my parents decided to buy a house on the beach instead of a cleaner, larger, newer house to replace the one I grew up in. Our house in the city was surrounded by heavy traffic, alcoholics, poverty-stricken families who had just arrived from South Carolina, Mississippi, and Alabama, and an assortment of characters who made my travels around school, the library, church, and stores a living hell. The boys at the beach were generally nice and they took me for rides in the speed boats that their parents were happy to give them as Christmas or birthday presents when they turned twelve. My girdle successfully foiled a seduction maneuver by one of them in his front passenger seat. Almost everybody in Columbia Beach caught crabs at the end of the pier that jutted out several hundred feet from the beach area, and the boys taught me how to catch crabs in huge metal square cages, the sides of which dropped open when the cages hit the sandy bottom of the Chesapeake Bay. The boys pushed me around in shoulder-deep water and tried to teach me to swim. One of them, Corbin, had kissed me on the lips.

About ten years my senior, Corbin lived down the street from our house at the beach. His father was a medical doctor and he had several siblings. A bulky six-footer, Corbin looked like a linebacker. The color of mahogany, he was sweet and shy. He followed me around for several months, talked to me softly about the university that he attended, and made me wonder what his pillowy lips tasted like.

The main reason we were ensconced at the beach house was that my mother had started an affair with a real-estate agent, Mr. Wise. A tall, courtly, light-skinned man, he lived across the street from us with his sickly wife, who rarely left home. While my father worked three jobs in the city, all of the children lived with my mother at the beach house, about an hour away by car. Mama's affair with Mr. Wise was so intense that I was left to care for my four siblings nearly every night. Thus, our first kiss occurred at the front door, on the patio.

His lips were so soft, smooth, and squishy that I could hardly feel them. I was too inexperienced to seek out the teeth and tongue behind them, and he was too much of a gentleman to introduce me to them. I was content to brush my mouth against his and wonder, while my lips traveled across his face, how a man's skin could possibly be so tender. How many times I kissed Corbin after that first encounter I do not recall, but I do know that it was never enough.

In spite of my varied encounters with water in adolescence, I did not learn to swim until I was nearly thirty years old. To my dismay, I had discovered that I was not a natural swimmer, that I sank like a rock if I did not pay attention, and that my strongest stroke was on my back with my chin pointed at the ceiling or sky. This technique also prevented my eyes from stinging in the highly chlorinated pool at the YWCA, where I took swimming lessons. By the time I boarded the bus with my fellow law-school professor, I was a strong swimmer who could snorkel for hours. I had one good stroke and no fear of the water.

I took the last available seat on the shabby bus and shared it with a large, light blue metal box that was spotted with rust. When we had traveled a few miles, I peered at it closely and spied a skull and crossbones emblazoned on two sides. Inspection of the third side revealed a detailed rendering of a huge snake with fangs exposed. It was the container for snake-bite treatments. I began to have a bad feeling about the adventure. Maybe it had not been a good idea to sign the ten-page waiver stating that anything that might go badly was my fault for having agreed to the trip. That feeling got worse as the bus wheezed to the top of the mountain, and I felt trapped in the rattling, shaking, bone-jarring, crusty old vehicle. We emerged from the bus and gathered around three weather-beaten guides who were dressed in rags and sandals.

In the hour just before dawn, the Rio Grande Gorge turned out to be a cliff that stretched as far as the eye could see. At the base of the cliff was a ribbon of water that crashed against boulders and promptly disappeared around a sharp corner. On the far side of the ribbon was another cliff. At the bottom of the gorge, the Rio Grande looked like a satin, platinum cloth that had cut through sheer brown rock as if it were a pile of sugar. It had created the Rio Grande Gorge, and we were at the headwaters of the river, where snowmelt cascaded to form falls that stretched for miles. We would enter the falls in rubber rafts that looked like broken balloons, and we would emerge at the base of the gorge where the ancient bus would meet us again. The trip would take a full day.

The head guide, a bow-legged pony-tailed hippie who never stopped grinning, gave a speech that had three parts. "First, I am happy to take all of you out today, because it is the very first rafting trip of the season," he said. "The snow's just melted and the river will get much deeper as more snowmelt flows through the gorge in late spring. We'll map and record any new boulders that may have crashed into the water during the winter." My mind translated this into: "The water is ice cold and these men have no idea what lurks around each river bend." Next, the guide emphasized what to do in the "unlikely" event that the raft capsized or we fell into the water. "The most important rule is 'Do not let go of the paddle.' The paddle is to be held across the chest, like this, while you swim on your back with your toes sticking up out of the water so that your feet do not get tangled in a tree branch or a rock. You must swim to the middle, deepest part of the river and always swim with the top of your head pointed downstream, never upstream." I translated this to mean, "Do not fall into the water, and good thing I can swim on my back pretty well, and the paddle might save my life." Finally, the guides showed us how to put on our wet suits and how to paddle so that the raft would be propelled safely down the gorge.

We hiked to the raft. By the time we climbed aboard the bouncy craft, I had convinced myself that the broken noses, facial scars, and maimed fingers and toes of the guides meant nothing. I figured all would be well. When we rounded the first bend, we discovered that all the large rock formations that confronted us in the middle of the river had horrific names, like "Screaming Mary," the "Devil's Cauldron," and "Hell Rock." At the next bend, the guide cheerfully informed us about the idiosyncratic nature of the rubber raft. "See, what all rubber rafts want to do with rocks in their path is *not* to bounce around them like a ball. No, what the raft wants to do with a big rock, say thirty-feet high, like this one here, is what a spider wants to do with a wall. The raft wants to climb the rock. Then, when it gets to the top of the rock, the raft wants to flip over. So, your job and my job is to keep the raft from climbing these here rocks." We soon discovered that our raft was no exception to this general rule.

For some reason, all ten of us, including the guide in our raft, thought this turn of events was hilarious. It is possible that the mania of the guide at the rear of our particular raft was contagious, like some hideous virus. We enthusiastically and vigorously paddled to ensure that no part of the raft touched a huge boulder as the current propelled us swiftly downriver. When the raft did touch a boulder, I was dispatched to the front of the raft because I was the smallest person onboard and because I volunteered happily to do it. There, I sat on the very edge of the raft and gleefully bounced up and down to dislodge the craft before it could inch its way to the top of the rock. On our way downriver, this occurred about four times as the swift current hurled us onto the jagged protuberances, but our luck was about to change.

About halfway down the gorge, the river slammed the raft into the tallest boulder we had encountered so far on the adventure. It was close to the base of the cliff, which rose several hundred feet straight up out of the water. A sliver of bright blue sky appeared between it and the matching cliff on the opposite side of the swirling water. As soon as the raft collided with the forty-foot high boulder, it began to rapidly ascend it. I assumed my position and began to bounce for all I was worth in an effort to dislodge the raft, while my fellow boaters used their paddles to steer back to the middle of the foaming river. In my excitement, I failed to notice that the raft had become vertical too quickly. Soon, when the raft flipped over into the Rio Grande, the laws of physics required that I be propelled through space like a pebble released from a slingshot.

"Now I am going to die," I thought calmly as I sailed through the air in a high arc aimed toward the rock-strewn water. I was not afraid yet. I hit the water with the top of my head and sank to the bottom like a stone. My clothing consisted of a pair of laced-up tennis shoes, no socks, a spandex bodysuit, a tee shirt, a neoprene wetsuit top, a life-preserver jacket, and a dark blue Red China cotton Mao cap with a red metal star sewn on the front. My boyfriend had given it to me from his trip to Red China the year before. When my head hit the water, I felt my forehead graze a rock so softly that it felt like a kiss. Later, I would find a tiny scratch just above my nose. A few vigorous kicks brought me up to the surface and I found myself in the middle, deepest part of the water. The raft and my fellow travelers were nowhere in sight.

Soon, I was swimming on my back with my chin and toes pointed skyward. When I inspected myself for blood and injuries, I discovered to my surprise that I was clutching the paddle in my right hand. Smiling broadly at my good luck in maintaining control of it, I figured that the paddle would lead to my rescue pretty soon. While the swift current carried me relentlessly down the river, my expertise with my only good stroke enabled me to avoid several large rocks in my path. When my feet began to go numb from the near-freezing water, I began to panic but, at that exact point, I saw one of the guides standing alone on a pile of rocks nearby. He was searching for me. I smiled at him and shouted. He motioned for me to swim toward him and said something that the roar of the water muffled. At a distance of about twenty yards from him, I could finally make it out. He was pointing at me and shouting, "The paddle!" He reached out toward me.

He was going to save my life by helping me get out of the deadly, icy cauldron via the paddle, of course. That was why the guide had made us promise to hold on to the paddle if we got dunked. The paddle was my lifesaver. Taking great care not to become wedged in the rocks at the guide's feet, I slowly swam closer to him and extended the paddle toward him with my right arm. As I expected, he took hold of the paddle. But, instead of using it to guide me and my numb legs to safety, the guide gave a mighty tug and wrenched it from the death grip of my numb right fist, nearly capsizing me in the process. Upon retrieval of the paddle, he turned his back on me and began clambering swiftly back up the slippery rocks, out of harm's way.

All alone once more, I floated in the shallow water near his feet. My hopes for a speedy rescue had been dashed. "What about *me*?" I shouted. "What am I supposed to do *now*?" He turned to me. "Swim back out to the middle of the river," he shouted at me above the howling water. "Go downstream, around the next bend. About a hundred yards beyond the bend, you'll see a small area of sand, about five feet across, at the base of the cliff. Swim on your back to that sandy area and wait for us there. We'll turn the raft over and bring it down to pick you up." It seemed an impossible task but there was no point arguing about it, since he had already resumed his trek across the rocks. I would have been arguing with a retreating back.

By the time I dragged myself onto the narrow, sandy shoreline, numbness had reached my waist, my teeth were chattering so hard that I thought they would break, and my entire body was wracked with painful, shivering spasms. There were no dry clothes for me to change into but, fortunately, it was a hot, sunny day with no wind. Eventually, the guides were able to wrestle the undamaged raft right-side up, and they paddled to the beach with all the other soaked passengers inside it. None of us was injured, although three men had been trapped beneath the raft when it capsized. Since I was the only one who had been catapulted, I was the only one who had to be rescued from the shoreline, several miles downstream.

There was no way to avoid it. I stood on the only shore, which was two feet across, and the cliffs rose hundreds of feet on both sides of the river. The only way out of the gorge was to get back in the raft and paddle to the pick-up point at the base of the mountains. Climbing back into the craft, I wondered aloud where my Red China cap was. I had been wearing it when I took the plunge. About ten miles downriver from the sand, I saw it, floating serenely in the middle of the water. A guide snagged it with a paddle. When I placed it on my still-soggy head, I figured that was where my body would have been if I had come just a little closer to the rock that had kissed my forehead on the way down.

A few hours later, we all took our seats in the old bus as cold beers were passed around for all of us, including the guides. We sipped or guzzled the bottles and one of the guides proposed a toast. His sandals had been strapped to his feet with Velcro and, when the raft capsized, the river had claimed one of them. Since he was not the one who had claimed my paddle, he was my favorite. On my way to the patch of sand, I had realized that the cost of replacing the paddle was the reason for the need to hold on to it. Of all the moments of crippling fear that day, it was my utter disappointment following the snatching of the paddle that caused me the most anguish later, when the inevitable flashbacks occurred. The toast that the guide had us drink to as we left the Rio Grande Gorge behind was, "Here's to cheating death, once again."

# Scene Twenty-Three
## Graduation Day

How had Kim managed to talk me into this? I was walking from Somerville to Cambridge, Massachusetts, carrying a sleeping two-year-old child to my daughter's college graduation, and I was not happy. My daughter had announced that she would not return to complete her senior year at college unless she could live off-campus. She had identified a satisfactory roommate and the two of them lived in a sun-drenched newly-renovated two-bedroom apartment on an old shaded street in Somerville, one town over from the campus.

When I asked my daughter what she needed for the apartment, she described a portable television set, which was on sale at an appliance store nearby. Although I knew that my daughter did not watch television, I bought it anyway, and helped her carry it down the street. Perhaps the capability of showing a video on repeat was the selling point, but Mitch owned no movies. When I saw the project that the roommate had submitted for part of her master's degree, I discovered why I had purchased the set. The roommate, a diminutive Asian woman with an angelic face, had videotaped herself as she painstakingly sealed herself inside a clear plastic box. The film began with her sitting on the floor smoking a cigarette while surrounded by clear plastic squares and a portable heat-sealing gun. One square was beneath her hips. She raised each pane of plastic around her body and heat-sealed it to the next square along the edge. At the end of the film, she was seated inside the sealed square with her face resting on her knees and her arms wrapped around her legs while she smoked the cigarette down to a butt. As the tape played over and over, the viewer was nearly hypnotized by her contortions and the banality of it all.

The toddler I carried was Kim's, and she was sleeping because she had spent the entire preceding night wailing like a banshee. During the ten-hour drive from Washington, D.C., the pelting rain had lulled her into a peaceful state. Although awake, Erika had presented no problem until we reached our destination in Somerville. My daughter, her roommate, and the roommate's tiny family had vacated the apartment for the graduation ceremony near dawn. Kim, her daughter, and I had started out much later, and we were in danger of being too late. The problem was that Kim had worn the wrong shoes. Her dainty pink sandals matched her suit, but she could not walk two blocks in them, much less two miles to the next town. She had to change into her combat boots, which were in the car, parked more than six blocks away in the other direction.

Erika was howling on the sidewalk as her mother explained the dilemma. Kim, my niece, was Chee Chee's second daughter. Due to mental illness, my sister had been unable to care for her from birth. My mother had taken Kim out of foster care at age six, "because she was so cute," but by the time Kim turned twelve Mama had begun to realize that she was unable to raise the child herself. After the police and child services had been called too often, I finally agreed to take Kim into my home, when she was in high school.

Unfortunately, my efforts to convince Kim to attend college full time had failed, but she had nearly obtained a hairdresser license by the time she gave birth to two children so close together that they looked like twins. Kim and my daughter had shared a home together for several years, and Kim was determined to attend Mitch's graduation. While Kim made the trip, she had nobody to care for the temperamental little girl, so Kim persuaded me to ride as a passenger in the car Kim drove up for Harvard's graduation. I knew that Erika would stop crying as soon as she lost sight of her mother, as she had established that pattern about a year before. Kim laughed when I told her that her daughter was happiest when she was not around. Maybe she didn't believe me.

Sure enough, as soon as Kim turned the corner to retrieve her boots, the baby stopped crying. I was not surprised by that, but what she did next did surprise me. She fell asleep on her feet as we walked toward Cambridge. Since the child was about to fall on her face, I picked her up and began jogging in the direction of the campus. I was not alone, for the entire population of Somerville seemed to be headed in the same direction, since there was no parking allowed anywhere near the site of the graduation. Exhausted and drenched in sweat, I once again cursed my daughter's choice of schools.

It was all my fault. After all, I was the one who had allowed her to attend Capitol Hill Day School when she had refused to return to the Montessori school that I had chosen. At Capitol Hill Day School, her grooming by teachers for entrance into Harvard University had begun, based on her ridiculously high standardized test scores in every area. The grooming had continued at Sidwell Friends High School, where I sent her for the best education. When she was given early admission, I had allowed her to attend Harvard University because her father and all her teachers thought it would be best for her. She turned down full scholarships from several top universities, including Howard University, the alma mater of her father and me. When I told her that she would be entering the belly of the beast at Harvard, she just laughed.

I was angry as I approached the gate. Mitch had barely survived four years at the university but she still wanted to raise her grade point average by remaining as an undergraduate student for an additional year or two. We had argued about it the previous semester and I finally made it clear that she could do that, but I would not contribute another cent to her education if she did. Because her father and I made too much money, Harvard had only given her a pittance in loan money and I had taken out two mortgages on the Southwest townhouse for her tuition payments. I am not very good at budgets.

At the last minute, Mitch had relented. She would graduate with her entering class. When I walked through the gate, I recalled that

I still had Kim's entry ticket in my purse. Security was tight, and the site was surrounded by fences and armed guards. A young blonde in a guard's uniform stood at the first barrier. I showed her the two tickets for admission and pressed one of them into her hand, explaining quickly what had happened with Kim. "Give this ticket to my niece, Kim, when she walks up to the gate," I requested. "She is about six feet tall, looks mixed, but she is black, a little lighter than her daughter here. She is huge, and she will be wearing a fuzzy pink suit and black combat boots." The young woman agreed to give Kim the ticket and I walked in a straight line past the fence. As soon as I got beyond the fence, I saw that the graduation ceremony was opening with the graduates marching toward their seats. Gazing at the sea of tassels, robes, and sandals, I felt a thud in my chest like I had gotten punched from the inside. A sob tore from my throat and my eyes stung with tears. In an instant, I began crying hysterically. My brain caught up with my emotions. "My baby is graduating from college!" it shouted to me over and over.

It was a feeling of relief like I had never experienced before, and it almost knocked me down. A weight flew from my shoulders and I stood straight up and nearly bounced on my toes. I laid the sleeping girl gently on the grass at my feet, and I tried to wipe the blinding tears away, but they would not disappear. The sobs made me double over. White strangers rushed over and asked me whether I was okay. "I'm crying from happiness," I said, and they understood. Kim found me and her sleeping daughter about two hours later. "How did you get past the gate?" I asked when I saw her waving. Kim looked at me, wrinkled her nose, and poked out her mouth. "Why this white-woman guard ask me if I was Kim?" she demanded. "She gave me a ticket. How she know my name?" I laughed hysterically. The main speaker was Conan O'Brien, a brilliant new late-night talk-show host and a Harvard University alumnus. I laughed hysterically some more. Then, I found Mitch and cried again. The whole day was a blur because I spent it thinking about what a terrible mother I had been.

I had never meant to be a terrible mother, of course. No woman ever does. When I made the decision to get pregnant and have a child, I was motivated mainly by curiosity and by the fact that my reproductive organs were thirty-two years old. I knew that I lacked the temperament and patience to raise a mentally or physically challenged child, so I had amniocentesis to make sure the baby was normal. I knew that I would continue to practice law, so I hired a live-in nanny. And I knew that I wanted to breast feed my baby, so I took three months off from work to ensure that I could properly care for my baby right after her birth. I read every book on infants and child care that I could buy or borrow. I fired my doctor and found a new one who promised to give me no medication during childbirth unless I specifically requested it. Finally, I went to La Maze classes to ensure that no drugs or complications would harm the baby during birth, and I pestered Walter to buy an infant seat that would fit in the Porsche. What I did not know was that everything would fall apart and that I would be consumed by fear and guilt.

Things started falling apart when I went into labor. The instructor had failed to warn me that my advanced age, excellent muscle tone, and the fact that I had experienced no pregnancies, no abortions, and no births meant that the changes in the cervix would take longer to complete for birth and that the process would be especially excruciating. That meant double contractions. Nothing could have prepared me for the hours of mind-numbing agony that accompanied the birth. I was tied inside a church bell that was eight-feet high, and a monster was banging on the bell so hard that my entire mind and body vibrated with each blow. I was pinned inside a drum that a mad person played with abandon. The pain was so acute and the waves so swift that none of my remaining senses could function. I was rendered blind, deaf, and dumb, so that I could feel each thud of my cervix more acutely as it slowly dilated. But the worst was yet to come.

In the hospital after the delivery, I was seized by two powerful emotions that I could not ignore. The first was fear, so compelling that it nearly paralyzed me. I feared for the safety of the baby with such strength that it almost canceled out the second emotion, which was a love so new and profound that I could barely stand to look at the newborn girl, because I melted inside. Even though I was exhausted from the grueling hours of labor, I insisted that she stay in my room. No bottle could touch her perfect lips, and I would begin breastfeeding immediately. The hospital was too filthy for her. I had to take her home as soon as possible. On the way home, things fell apart. The infant seat had not been properly installed and I ranted and raved until we reached the townhouse we had just bought for the baby. When I stepped through the door, I got another shock. Walter had been home alone for three days and the entire house was strewn with newspapers, unwashed dishes, and spoiled food. It would be impossible to live with him and the baby in the same house.

In a hormonal funk, I had called him from my private room in the hospital and begged him to spend the night with me, in the corner bed that had been thoughtfully provided for proud fathers. He refused my request because it was inconsistent with the Lillian he knew. I never forgave him for this act of abandonment, or for his refusal to take paid sick leave or annual leave from his government job to help me and the nanny cope with the tsunami that was Mitch.

For three months, I nursed on demand, quickly losing the fifty pounds I had gained during the pregnancy. Although the baby had her own room, I had her bassinette moved into the master bedroom so that I could comfort her when she cried. Like an earthquake or a hurricane, my daughter became a force of nature and I was powerless to resist. When I returned to work, it was even more horrible. My imagination tortured me with all the terrible things that could happen to her without my presence and protection. After I rushed home, a crippling fear gave way to a love so obsessive that I rushed her to the doctor when she had three pimples on her tummy from what I suspected was chicken pox. The doctor looked at me rather strangely. "This is the earliest I have ever seen symptoms," he mumbled. So that she would not scratch the bumps and scar her skin, I used a razor blade to slice open edible vitamin E capsules and dabbed the syrup on each of the eighteen bumps that erupted during the course of the disease.

By the age of four, Mitch had developed several tiny bumps around her eye area. A visit to a specialist produced the bad news that it was a virus, which was spreading closer to her eyes each month. The virus might disappear on its own or, in several years, it might reach the point where it would cause blindness. There was no cure. The only procedure available was the excision of each bump, all the way to its root beneath the skin, accomplished only with a scalpel. She was too small for anesthesia or painkillers and, when the doctor attempted the procedure, Mitch jerked her head involuntarily. Several times, the doctor almost jabbed her in the eye with the sharp instrument. In frustration, he gave up, musing that we would just have to wait and see. I asked whether there was any alternative, a habit I have acquired when given a scenario I do not like. "Yes, there is," he said. "You could do it at home. Take this curette and sterilize it. You must dig out every part of each bump. If you leave any, they will grow back again very soon. If she is relaxed and if she trusts you, she may allow you to do it, but you must have a steady hand, because most of these are very close to her eyeball. It may leave some scarring, but that is a chance worth taking. I am sure you will agree." Mitch allowed me to do what she refused to permit in the doctor's office. The virus was eliminated and it never returned. She has no recollection of the procedure at my hands.

Before Mitch's first birthday, I had a plan. I was a terrible mother and her father was a great parent. My fears for her safety and my emotional attachment to her felt unnatural and overwhelming to me. My curiosity had caused me to give birth to a baby that I was unable to raise, and I believed that I was going to ruin her life with my anxiety and guilt. Before her birth, I could ignore Walter and escape into my own world of sex, sports, books, music, and work. But, with the baby in my life, I had to interact with Walter so that the two of us could parent her. I could not live with the two of them, so I decided that I would leave both of them. Across the street from the townhouse was an apartment building where Walter and I lived before Mitch was born. I would move into that building as soon as she was weaned to a cup. Knowing that I had a plan—and that I would soon escape—made the first year of the baby's life bearable, but I endured those months in a post-partum, hormone-addled state of panic and obsession.

The plan worked. I moved into a rented apartment and left them to their own devices. The problem was that, every day after work, my feet carried me into the townhouse and to my daughter. I did not want to be there, but I would supervise her dinner, allow her to spill food all over my silk blouse, and stay until her father came home from work. Soon, I was taking her back to my apartment with me, because I could not bear to leave her behind. I was a terrible mother. I had a problem letting go. A few months later, I solved the problem by divorcing Walter, buying him out of the house, and getting joint custody of Mitch. Thus began her childhood of two homes and of shuttling back and forth between the terrible mother who could not let her go and the father who was clueless.

By the time Mitch had reached the age of fifteen, I again concluded that she would be better off without me. The law totally fascinated me and I was unable to stop myself from putting in the eighty-hour workweeks that seemed to creep up on me. When working on the Hill, my Senate Judiciary Committee duties often required me to pick up Mitch from the after-school program at six PM and take her back to my office, where she ran through the marble halls as if demons were chasing her until nine or ten PM. Later, when working on appellate briefs, time stood still for me but

Mitch knew, when she woke herself up on Saturday morning and found me still working, that I had been sitting at the dining room table, poring through transcripts for twelve hours straight. All too often, criminal trial work required me to bring her along to crime scenes, witness interviews, and court appearances. I feared that, in the constant war between the law and my child, the law had won many more battles.

When she was fourteen years old, Mitch began to stay out half the night. She went to raves—illegal, white, under-age parties that moved from one seedy venue to another every week. One of the cool kids, she partied with older friends from Sidwell Friends High School and other private schools in the area, and she started smoking cigarettes, which were not allowed in my presence. I raided her room and her backpack regularly to confiscate the cigarettes and the matches that she brought home. It was impossible to enforce a curfew with her, but she remained a straight-A student. Her father had remarried, to a woman Mitch despised, and Mitch was distancing herself from him. It had taken me two years to get appointed as a federal administrative law judge. Because I was unable to budget money, the only way I could have a retirement income was to leave private practice and return to federal service, so I would be entitled to my pension under the old civil-service retirement system, which I had entered in 1973. The easiest way to do that was to take the posting for a federal administrative law judge that was available in Fresno, California. Mitch did not want to relocate with me, so I escaped, leaving her with her father for the second time in her life. She would be fine without me. She had her friends and, in a few years, she would be in college.

I had been in Fresno for less than a month when the telephone calls started. Mitch wanted to visit. When she came to Fresno, I could tell that she was losing weight and that she was depressed. My daughter missed me, and I missed her too. I had made a mistake leaving my baby again, and I had to get back home to her. I was invited to apply for a promotion that would bring me back to the East Coast, in New Haven Connecticut. My office in Fresno had no computer or computer hook-up because my predecessor judge had refused to use one. The attorney-writers who assisted in drafting the technical final decisions were backed up by three months. When the supervising attorney ushered me into the room containing the backlog, I saw files that could not fit in the allotted file cabinets. Instead, they covered tables, chairs, desks, and the floor. Instantly, the room reminded me of two law offices I had seen in the past. The first belonged to a solo practitioner who needed a law clerk. His office, in a commercial strip on Capitol Hill, had grown from one room to three, and each room contained a desk, chairs, and a sofa. All of these surfaces were buried under case files that cascaded to the floor. His filing system was simple. "When one room gets filled with files, I rent another one," he explained. Although he claimed to know where each client file rested, I did not believe him. The second office I had seen in a similar state was Walter's at the SEC. I had foolishly offered to help him with his backlog when he began to whine incessantly about his own procrastination. One weekend, he took me up on the offer. When he opened the office door, I saw that stacks of bound documents covered not just the furniture, but every inch of the floor, as well. It was a black hole for paperwork that he was paid to review. I closed the door quietly and silently walked out of the suite, wondering why he still had a job. I wanted to be the number one applicant for the New Haven promotion so, in four months, I had to increase the Fresno office's number of trials and written decisions. To accomplish my goal, I worked sixteen-hours a day, every day of the week, for four months. During that time, I broke two permanent bridges in my lower jaw, overdosed myself on hormones, lost half the hair on my head, and gained twenty pounds. Then I moved to New Haven, Connecticut.

Though I was back on the East Coast, Mitch's calls continued, but worse. Sobbing on the other end of the telephone, Mitch insisted that

I return to Washington, D.C. Her visits to New Haven—like her visits to Fresno—showed weight loss and stress. Her grades were also plummeting to B's for the first time. I had to come home. In five months, I took the New Haven Social Security Hearing Office from last place in production in the region to first place. My reward was a recommendation for a vacancy in the Securities and Exchange Commission's administrative law judges office in Washington, D.C. I could come home.

I moved back into the townhouse with my daughter. Her rave days seemed to be behind her, her grades improved, and she ran cross country in her senior year. Although I tried to talk her out of it, Mitch insisted on attending Harvard. I was a terrible mother, so I let her do it.

# Scene Twenty-Four
## Goodbye, Mama

My good friend, Burt, whom I met at the Securities and Exchange Commission, was physically repugnant for many reasons. He had chronic bad breath, but he refused to chew the gum that I offered him every time I was in his presence. Half the time, he refused the mints that I kept in my wallet just to offer to him. Claiming that deodorant irritated his sensitive skin, he also refused to wear it to eliminate his powerful perspiration odor. I purchased about six different brands of deodorant from health food stores and, when I gave them to him, I ordered him to find one that he liked and buy it for himself in the future. He accepted them and then disobeyed my orders.

Burt's entire body was covered with long, silky hairs and, whenever they touched me, they gave me the creeps because they felt like tiny spiders. On the few occasions that we slept together, I wore a full-length silk gown or two-piece, long-sleeved pajamas to ensure that the hairs did not touch me. When I discovered that his fine, dark-red hair looked weird because he was trimming it himself, I sent him to a barber for a pre-paid haircut on his birthday.

A cowboy-boot-wearing baseball fan, Burt stood well over six-feet tall. The most prominent feature of his large frame was a protruding backside that had made him the victim of merciless teasing throughout his childhood years. Idyllic summer camp sun exposure had left him with skin cancer that erupted as small nodules on unpredictable parts of his face. These eruptions were scraped off and gouged out to create large scars that gave sweet Burt a rugged appearance that I adored. One of his legs was shorter than the other, perhaps from undiagnosed childhood polio, and he wore a lift in his shoe, but he had a rolling John Wayne-type way of walking. An avid horseman, Burt was the closest thing to a cowboy that I ever knew. He flirted shamelessly with any woman with a pretty feature, including her smile.

Burt was pretty much impotent, due to an inability to sustain an erection, and I was not willing to assist him in solving the problem. Thus, I was always happy when a new female interest appeared in his life. Eventually Burt asked if he could move into my townhouse. He had been living in a small, one-bedroom apartment since his wife divorced him several years earlier and he was lonely. When I told him yes, on the condition that both of us could continue to see others romantically, he turned down the offer and continued his search for true love. He wanted to retire from federal service by age seventy, and he wanted to share his retirement years with someone who loved him. Like most of us past the age of sixty, Burt talked about retirement plans incessantly.

It started as a slight cough, and Burt was a good patient. He submitted to the tests that his doctors scheduled and he took a succession of allergy medications, hoping that the next one would work. When the cough turned into a slight gurgle, I knew that he had to do something different. My theory was that my buddy had tuberculosis, and I nagged him until he scheduled an x-ray with a new doctor.

When I first met Burt, he was sitting in his office at the Securities and Exchange Commission. He would vacate the office in a few days—when I was appointed to replace him—while Burt would return to his old assignment at the Department of Transportation. He had been at the SEC for less than six weeks when he realized that his new chief judge would make his life a living hell. Burt had known her before her appointment to the position of chief administrative law judge, and he was so shocked at the transformation in her personality that he had to leave the SEC. When he asked his old chief for his job back, he got an enthusiastic response.

Unlike Burt, I had been warned about the problems that the chief judge would present and I was prepared for them, I thought. More importantly, the appointment at the SEC was the quickest way for me to get back to my daughter, who was miserable at her father's house. After the first encounter with Burt in our office, I came to rely on him for sound advice, dinner, lunches, trips to the movies, symphonies and operas, and shopping for suits, dresses, shoes, and silk blouses. I married another man and divorced him while I remained close to Burt. When Burt scheduled the x-ray, he had been married for a year to his new wife, and we were still close.

The only thing that came between me and Burt was the cancer that the film revealed in his lung and liver. Less than six months after his diagnosis, Burt was dead. While he and I spent frequent lunches talking about death and the meaning of life, Burt's new wife embarked on a renovation of her suburban house that was so extensive they had to move into a nearby apartment building for several weeks. She was making the house wheelchair accessible for what she thought would be his recuperation and remission. Although Burt had lived most of his life as a practicing Jew, and I was an atheist for most of my life, we discovered over our ten-year friendship that we were more like each other than we were like our own family members. We learned from each other. He taught me about Judaism and I taught him about slavery in America, and we laughed a lot, mostly at ourselves. When we met at Union Station for what would be our last restaurant lunch, Burt sat opposite me in a booth with an oxygen tank beside him and a nozzle stuck up his nose. But I still loved talking to him, and I knew he was there because he loved me. He laughed at all my jokes and swore that I was smarter than him. We agreed that Mitch was smarter than both of us.

On the day of Burt's funeral, my lover Abdul was my houseguest for the weekend. Although I knew that Burt's funeral service was to be held in a synagogue, and Abdul was a practicing Muslim, I invited him to accompany me. He graciously agreed. When we entered the main room and saw all the covered heads, Abdul calmly accepted the proffered skullcap and donned it. As soon as I got seated, the tears burst forth, shocking me and Abdul. When the tears continued at the gravesite, Abdul gave me his pristine handkerchief and I realized that I was not just crying for Burt, but also for my father. Burt was only seven years older than me and my father had been dead for more than fifteen years.

I did not cry at my father's funeral, but I did get drunk at the repast. Even worse, I laughed out loud at the funeral Mass. My older brother, who made the funeral arrangements, had brought some of us family members to the rectory to meet his parish priest. The housekeeper, a flaming diva gay man, opened the rectory door. When the parish priest made his entrance, all I saw was a rotund, short man in the closet. My teenaged niece, Kim, was living with me at the time, and when I got home I told her, "I'm pretty sure that the priest who will say the funeral Mass is gay, Honey." Then I forgot about the subject. But, the next day, when the priest emerged from the sacristy to begin the Mass, his mincing steps and effeminate gestures gave him away. I felt Kim, in the pew behind me, tap on my left shoulder. "Ooh," she whispered, filling my left ear. "Why he a faggy, Aunt Lillian— just like you say?" The observation struck me as hysterically funny, and I had to bend over and hide my face so that I could not be seen laughing at my father's funeral Mass. When the service was over, dozens of church members singled me out to offer their heartfelt sympathy. I had recited a poem that I wrote but I had not shed a tear, and I did not figure out what my heaving shoulders must have looked like until several days after the burial.

This is how my poem looked on the last page of the funeral program:

*A part of my soul has been missing since Sunday.*
*Gone to the place where kisses and tears live on*
*After they have been ours to spend too freely or too sparingly.*
*Now tell me how he loved me – was it*
*Waffles on Sunday, candy in his pockets,*
*Cameras and flashbulbs, let's have dinner next week,*
*A check now and then, a smile when he saw me?*
*My heart is filled with footprints.*
*His fingerprints brushed our brains.*
*We were marked with part of his being*
*In our struggle to please, each in our own way.*
*There will be no forgetting him.*
*But the goal eludes us now*
*And we can never satisfy Daddy.*
*You took Daddy away on Sunday.*

My father's death at age ninety-three had been preceded by a bad fall that had broken his pelvis. He had fallen while residing at a fancy nursing-home-type assisted-living facility that I had fought hard to keep him out of. When he decided to move out of his efficiency apartment in Southwest Washington, D.C., I started a campaign to get him to live in my house. I knew that I did not love him, but I had become obsessed with the desire to have him spend the last few years of his life in the company of his family and with the need to have him die in the presence of people who knew him.

Although he had steadfastly refused to visit my nearby home unless several other siblings were also present, my father and I had made monthly visits to my brother Tony, when he was institutionalized at Saint Elizabeth's Hospital over the years. The two of us sat across the table in the recreation area and told my brother the family news and asked him, "How is the food here?" and, "When was the last time you went for a walk?" and similar questions. Tony's side of the conversation consisted of gibberish in a mixture of school-boy Spanish and made-up words that had common themes of religion and imagined travels. On rare occasions, my brother recalled a family member's name and inquired specifically about that person. Diagnosed with schizophrenia as a teenager, Tony had wandered all over the East Coast. We also visited my older sister, Chee Chee, in the same institution, with pretty much the same results and conversations during a visit, except she did not make up words. Her diagnosis was the same, and her specialty was suicide attempts, not wandering.

My efforts to convince my father to live in my house were thwarted. Over the course of several weeks, my father made vague objections, such as "I need my privacy" or "I do not want to be a burden." I harassed him so much about my plans to cook for him and provide comfort and privacy downstairs that my siblings finally intervened. "Stop bothering him," they told me. "You are agitating him. Daddy is looking forward to moving into the facility. They will cook meals for him." The new facility was quite beautiful and I took Mitch to have dinner with her grandfather there several times. He had been living there only a few months when he fell. The broken pelvis developed complications and he lost the ability to walk. After being hospitalized, he was sent to a different facility and, shortly after his admission, he died there, in pain and alone, without family members around him.

At his funeral and burial, I pondered the same questions that had plagued me for so many years. I had asked him the question in many forms:

"Why were you so mean and cold when we were small?" He denied the choking, kicking, pinching, cursing, and criticism. He recalled no denial of food, no indifference to our well-being, and no threats of abandonment. Any cruelty I described was the fault of our mother, not him. After reaching adulthood, I had asked my mother the same questions and she gave me the same responses, except she specifically denied the whippings and blamed everything on my father. She also got angry. "Why are you always talking about the past?" she demanded. "Your father was no good. Why don't you just forget about that stuff? It was a long time ago. Everything is different now. I did the best I could. You should thank me. You have a wonderful life." Their refusal to apologize or to explain meant only one thing to me: They knew they were wrong when they did it, and they did it anyway. The tears I shed for my father on the day of Burt's funeral were tears for what might have been. Burt died in September 2006. Less than four months later, I retired from the federal government in January 2007. Working at the dysfunctional SEC would prove to be impossible without him.

When I retired, my mother was dying. I became obsessed with moving her into my house, just as I had with my father the year before his death. In response to my entreaties, my mother regularly called my house at three AM, sobbing and screaming that she wanted to move in and insisting that she would be ready to leave the next day. The next day, when I showed up, she would not leave her house. She changed her mind. What she wanted was for me to move into her filthy house with her and take care of her there. If I loved her, I probably would have. I lived alone, but my insistence to her and to my father grew out of duty, not emotional attachment. I had to force myself not to hate them for what they did to my older brother and sister while I watched. The nightmares that plagued me for decades did not allow me to forgive.

By the time my mother moved into my home, it was too late. Her dementia had progressed to the point where she had forgotten how to chew or swallow her food. An expert explained it to me a few months later: "Our instinct tells us only to place food in our mouths. It takes several months to learn to manipulate our tongues so that the food does not fall out and to coordinate our jaw muscles so that food gets masticated by the teeth. The process of swallowing is similarly complicated, so that food does not go down the wrong way and choke us." Mama also had a bed sore and she was incontinent. I knew these impairments were serious, but she was in no danger of falling in my house, where she could receive twenty-four-hour care while I continued to work. Shortly after her arrival, everything fell apart.

She slept on a new futon sofa bed downstairs so that she could get out of bed easily. She took her meals at a small table in front of the futon. Late at night, she was the most agitated and confused. Each night, she worked herself up into a mania about leaving my house and returning to her unlivable home on Randolph Place. Pacing and sitting on the toilet kept her up all night, but I had to sleep. To reduce the substantial risk of falls during the night, I hired a nurse's aide to help get my mother out of bed and onto the toilet. The bathroom was only five feet away, down the hall from where my mother slept. But, each night, I had to remind the aide to keep the dining table on the other side of the room at bedtime, so that my mother would not trip over it. Mama had also forgotten how to walk. I suspected that the nurse kept placing the table directly in front of the futon at night so that the noise of the furniture scraping against the marble tile floor would wake her from her forbidden sleep. One night, Mama bolted from the bed and crashed her head on the table edge, opening a narrow cut about an inch wide across her forehead. Because she was diabetic, it did not heal quickly.

Several days later, I had a brilliant idea. Mama had been surreptitiously spitting out her dementia medication onto the floor beside the table, and she was deteriorating. Maybe that was why she remained so delusional. If the pills were ground up and mixed with her soft food, I thought that might solve the problem. I had conquered my fear of blood and needles so that, when she became unable to inject herself, I could inject her with the insulin that her diabetes required. Now I could help to medicate the dementia. The aide and I finally succeeded in grinding four of the pills, and I had a rough idea of what one pill would look like in the mound that formed on the kitchen counter. The aide and I joked about administering the medication, and I walked out of the kitchen for a few minutes. When I returned, the white powder had disappeared. "What happened to the medication?" I asked. "I geev eet to thee Mama," she replied in her thick Caribbean accent. I knew she was not telling the truth, but I concluded that she simply thought that administering the pill in powder form was not a good idea. Instead of disagreeing with me, she had thrown the medicine away. I shrugged my shoulders. Maybe she was right, I figured as I left the kitchen.

The next day, I discovered that, in fact, when I left the kitchen, the aide had called my sister in a panic, telling her that I was planning to kill my mother with an overdose. My sister came to my house in the morning, saw the scab on my mother's head, and removed her from my house against my advice and protestations. My ranting and raving mother was placed in a suburban house run by religious zealots. In less than a month, she fell and broke her femur, and then several leg and hip fractures followed. Less than six months later, my mother was in great pain in a hospital with no family present and surrounded by strangers when she died of complications from the falls. In spite of my efforts, both of my parents had died alone. I did not cry at her funeral either. I read a monologue from Shakespeare's *Tempest* and felt only sadness for what might have been.

My mother died in May 2007, five months after my retirement. I was still grieving for Burt when I reached the hospital and was told that she had already died and that her body was locked up, ready to be transported to the morgue. My sister Pat and I ignored the nurses' orders and proceeded to my mother's room. On the bed was a thick, plastic black body bag, zipped up with a twist tie knotted at the top. Pat gasped beside me as I undid the twist tie and unzipped the bag. I have never feared death much. Inside was my mother's face, contorted in pain as I had seen her for the past several weeks. I kissed her cold cheek and whispered, "Goodbye, Mama." My sister did the same. Then I zipped up the bag, replaced the twist tie, and left the room, with Pat not far behind me.

A few days later, family members received a call from a group home in Philadelphia where my crazy brother Tony lived. He was very ill and near death. None of us had seen him for over five years, and he had not been informed of my mother's death or burial. When I got to the hospital in Philadelphia, I was too late. Alone in his hospital bed, Tony had died of undiagnosed cancer an hour before I arrived.

I entered the room and kissed his cold cheek. He looked just like his mother did when she lay in the body bag. Both of them had lost most of their hair and their teeth to the passage of time. "Listen, I have something important to tell you," I said to his lifeless face. "Mama died, and we buried her two days ago. Goodbye, Tony." I wrote a poem for him. Two weeks after my mother's burial, we scattered Tony's ashes over my parents' graves. That was when I wept for his wasted, tortured life. The last time I saw Tony alive, he was burrowing for food in a trash can on a crowded sidewalk in downtown Washington, D.C., more than ten years ago. I had crossed the street and walked swiftly away from him so that he would not recognize me.

# Scene Twenty-Five
## Did You Know?

"Did you know that your left leg is a half-inch shorter than your right?" I stared at the Beverly Hills Paul Newman lookalike plastic surgeon. I could not come up with an answer. The question brought back a flood of memories. In the alley behind our row house, I was eight years old. Somehow we had acquired a rusty, bluish boy's bicycle with squeaky handlebars and everybody in the alley could ride it and steer it except me. Although I was short, I was strong and well-coordinated, but I kept falling off and wobbling on the tattered leather seat. Eventually, I had to give up my turn and relinquish the two-wheeler to my siblings. The bike did not last long on our rough streets, but I was the only kid on the block who could not ride. I was also the only one who could not roller skate. We had one pair of metal skates, with a skate key for adjustments, but I was unable to maintain my balance for more than a few seconds and finally waved away my turns.

A half-inch shorter leg also meant that the Asian seamstress yelled at me to please "Sand up sate," so that she could hem the trousers or the skirt accurately. Spinning classes in the gym were impossible because I lurched from side to side at high speeds and got chafed from the friction generated by the seat. It also meant that my lovers told me I had a "pimp walk" or a "cripple walk" or a "distinctive walk" or "a limp." They had noticed something that I had ignored. One-half inch explained why one hip was concave and the other convex when I stood straight. Most importantly, it explained why I could not wear loafers, clogs, or backless high heels. I had to wear expensive, soft leather shoes with good support at the heel so that I could contort my feet when I walked. My mind was wandering. The plastic surgeon was examining me to determine what I wanted to change about my body. Really, I just wanted to put a big checkmark on a blank piece of paper and write "Everything" beside it, but I knew that made no sense. I was fifty-five years old, and I had to be sensible.

"No, I did not know that my left leg is shorter than my right," I finally answered. "How did it happen?" The surgeon smiled with the Paul Newman twinkle in his perfect eyes. "You were born that way," he explained. "Such a great deviation means that your back must hurt quite a bit. Does it?" I thought about the question. "No, it never hurts," I answered truthfully. "You must have somehow compensated for it in your gait," he said. "There is no need to correct it now, but you're very fortunate. Did you know that your nose was broken many years ago and that it healed crooked without medical treatment?" He smiled again. A new flood of memories assailed me.

I was twelve years old and my father had gone to work at his second job. My mother had gone dancing with her new boyfriend. The games began, and we each grabbed a favorite mop or broom. As I turned, one of my brothers broke his broom across my nose. The pain was crippling. I knew from experience that I had to put ice on it immediately and hold my head back to stop the bleeding. I also knew that the wound had to be kept secret. We would all be whipped without mercy if I had to be taken to the doctor. I accepted the pain and made myself invisible that night. "No," I lied to the plastic surgeon. "I don't recall my nose being broken. It must have happened when I was really young."

It was time to change the subject. "Why are my eyes so puffy in the morning?" I asked. He was happy to explain that, genetically, I had huge spaces in my facial area and these made it more likely that fluids would accumulate there instead of running down my throat at night. "Just sleep on your back instead of your stomach," he advised. "And you'll find that a lot of your problems with facial swelling and baggy eyes will be solved." This was good news. I decided not to tell him about the itch in my left eye that caused it to water. Though the itch was getting worse each month, what could a plastic surgeon do about an itchy eye? Maybe the new sleep posture would solve that problem too.

I was getting an assessment because I had always hated my body. I could not share this attitude with the plastic surgeon, for fear that he would send me to a psychiatrist instead of slicing or sucking away the hated parts. The request for elective surgery had to be made in terms of "feeling much younger than I look" or "matching up my body with the exercise that I do." Finally, we reached many compromises. "I advise against a tummy tuck because a little liposuction will suffice," he counseled me. "You do not need a bust lift. I would have to readjust your nipples for that and you would not like the scarring....I suggest removal of some excess from the sides if you want a different shape. A full facelift is not needed at this time...You do not have any wrinkles because you do not frown....You do not require drastic surgery around the eyes. Removal of a little tissue from under the eyelids top and bottom will solve those problems...."

After weeks of tests and preparation, the day of surgery arrived. I chose general anesthesia, and counted down to oblivion. I heard someone say, "She's out of it. She's under. Let's begin." Then a cacophony of voices punctuated the action. The surgeon had a surprise halfway through the procedure and asked everyone to "Come here and take a look at this!" Everybody said a collective "Ooh," and then the jumble of voices resumed for another hour. "She's awake now," I finally heard. "Get the doctor." I was still unable to move so I waited patiently, but I was unable to suppress a second moan. I was alive, but I wondered whether some weird cancerous growth had been discovered and sewn back up. That would account for the "Ooh" that I still recalled.

My girlfriend Myra would be coming to get me soon, and the doctor had to give me detailed instructions to ensure my rapid recovery. As I concentrated on the orders, I tried to forget about the cancerous growth and, soon, I was dressed and headed for the door. "By the way," the surgeon god said, looking at me curiously. "Your left eye must have been itching like the devil for some time, huh?" I was amazed at the question. "Yes!" I responded. "It was itching terribly for the past six months and it was getting worse. I thought it was my allergy acting up. Why do you ask, Doctor?" He twinkled. "Well, when I looked beneath your lower-left eyelid so that I could remove the fat deposit there, I found a very large skin tag that had been rubbing against your eyeball," he said. "It's the first time I have ever seen a skin tag in that particular position. I removed it surgically. It will not grow back any time soon. No additional charge. Just thought you might like to know."

He stood near the door, waiting for a response. Feigned ignorance is always appropriate when unsure of what to say. "Wow, Doctor!" I said. "That is amazing. What is a skin tag?" Since I knew the answer to my question, I did not have to listen to his short lecture. I decided not to tell him that I had heard him talking about his discovery during the operation and that I had feared that he had sewn up a cancerous growth. He would not have believed me.

# Scene Twenty-Six
## A Mean Man

Clarence and I were having an argument—a rare occurrence but the subject was serious. His grandfather was very ill and Clarence was expected to visit him before he died. The only bright spot in the childhood of Clarence and his brother was Tina, the grandfather's wife. She made sure the boys were well fed and tried to comfort them by making excuses for their maternal grandfather's abusive behavior. She explained that the grandfather was doing his best with them, and that he was simply unable to demonstrate his affection in any other way. His punches, slaps, whippings, and kicks were just his way of showing he cared. The curses, shouted orders, and verbal abuse were the only ways he could communicate. As the years passed, Clarence began to suspect that the old lady was wrong. By the time I met him, Clarence had become convinced that the cruelty of the grandfather was not an integral part of his personality but, rather, had been intentionally inflicted as a way to avenge himself on the boys' parents and the means by which he showed his neighbors how much better he was than them.

When Clarence brought his young son, Jamal, to visit Georgia, the old man treated the child like a prince, thinking that spoiling Jamal and interacting with him in front of Clarence would make up for his cruelty to Clarence. But this favored treatment revealed to Clarence another aspect of the old man's personality. It also stood in stark contrast to Clarence's own childhood experiences and made Clarence even more bitter to witness this new and improved version of the grandfather.

I understood Clarence's anger because I had seen the same behavior in my mother twice since the end of my own childhood. When I was seventeen years old, my mother gave birth to Manny, an infant with Down's syndrome. She boasted that she had refused the doctors' advice to allow the newborn to die in the hospital and that she ignored their predictions of his death by age two. I could not stand to listen to her talk about the baby, and I walked out of the room when he entered it. Manny never learned to talk and he shuffled when he walked.  My younger sister had the responsibility of caring for him but my mother issued the orders related to his feeding, maintenance, and medication. The deprivation of food that we experienced was replaced with abundance for Manny.

He was given so much to eat that, by the age of seven, he began to experience breathing problems and by eight he was wearing adult-sized clothing. By age nine, his clothes had to be custom ordered. He ate all day and all night. My sister was punished whenever Manny was not fed quickly enough. She soon developed great affection for him and they were inseparable. He followed her all over the  house, and he walked up and down the street in search of food. A series of hospitalizations preceded his death at age ten, when he weighed over two-hundred pounds. He could not walk ten yards without resting his massive bulk.

My parents divorced shortly after the death of Manny, with each blaming the other for his demise, but the solicitous behavior that my mother exhibited toward Manny continued when she took my niece Kim, at age six, from foster care to raise her. Kim grew from a normal size to morbid obesity in less than two years, as my mother demanded that she eat enormous restaurant meals paid for by her  boyfriend. When she brought the young, obese Kim to my home for a visit, she spent the evening telling the nine-year-old how  fat she was and forcing her to eat more food. My mother thought that feeding Manny and Kim demonstrated her capacity for affection and that paying attention to  them meant that she could be a good mother.

My mother and Clarence's grandfather were mistaken. Clarence and I both knew that they remained the same mean, cruel adults they had always been. Clarence refused to visit his sickly grandfather, in spite of my admonition that he might regret it one day. I told him that, in the future, he might regret not seizing this last opportunity to ask him questions and to find out how the grandfather felt about him. Clarence was firm. He had been a mean man, and Clarence did not want to see him. Although he had been nice to Jamal, that meant nothing. Clarence had a miserable childhood and nothing could change it. I lost the argument.

When the grandfather died shortly thereafter, in 1983, Clarence heaved huge sobs. I knew he was crying for what could have been a different relationship. Clarence had been abused and neglected over a number of years, but the grandfather was still a powerful figure in his life. Clarence thought that he had to attend the funeral, in Georgia. He refused my offer to accompany him, saying that he preferred to go by himself. Before he returned to Washington, D.C., I got a call from a vacationing girlfriend. She had passed through the Atlanta airport a few days earlier and happened to see Clarence, his wife, and his son there, arriving on a flight together.

*Me beside an ant hill with two children
in a Ugandan refugee camp in 2003.*

# Scene Twenty-Seven
## Where Is the Taptap?

The hugely pregnant young Ugandan woman was smiling so broadly in the headlights that her large chalk-white teeth gleamed and her round eyes disappeared into slits. "Thank you," she shouted over and over. "Thank you! Thank you!" With a final wave of her long slender fingers, she disappeared in the vicinity of the prison wall that ran along the right side of the narrow dirt road. I recognized her just as the truck was coaxed into first gear and the inky night swallowed her up. I had been in Uganda for a week, and this was my second day in the bush.

The American Bar Association had sent me to Uganda to assist in its initiative to enforce national legislation preventing child rape. When I visited a village the day before, I had been greeted as if I were a man. The village elders admired and respected me as a United States federal administrative law judge. The most beautiful village girls served me warm bottled sodas as they knelt beside my wooden stool in the common area outside the huts, and they kept their heads bowed to the dirt as the men conversed with me and with the female uniformed police lieutenant who was responsible for translating and for ensuring my safety.   Also responsible for my safety were six uniformed Ugandan soldiers who sported pistols on their hips and automatic rifles slung over their shoulders. I had to pay their commandant for their services before he would allow me to leave Kampala. Their neighbor, Congo, regularly raided the villages for food and soldiers, slaughtering women and children, so none of the roads outside the capital were safe. That cash transaction had taken a full day to consummate. The soldiers rode in the open bed of the truck, which the United Nations had donated the year before for child services. The truck conquered mud, rocks, and puddles of water to transport us from the capital city of Kampala, which straddled the equator, to the bush, where I would talk with children, police officers, and leaders about child rape and the rights of children.

The night before, refusing to abandon their post for the comfort of the beds inside, the stoic young soldiers had slept on the porch of a small hotel, called "The White House." When the power went out shortly after our arrival, the emergency generator switched on, but my panicky rush to the lobby in pitch darkness revealed that the generator was used only to ensure that the forty-two-inch flat-screen television in the bar continued to broadcast soccer matches. My room and the entire street outside were plunged into blackness while the match blared on. In the morning, I noticed that the security system consisted of jagged pieces of broken whiskey and soda bottles cemented onto the top of an eight-foot white wall. It protected the only object of value on the premises—a satellite dish measuring six-feet in diameter, perched precariously on the roof. I smiled.

The broken-glass security system at The White House Hotel reminded me of the security system in a hotel in Mali, which I had visited two years earlier. In the capital city of Bamako, I attended a conference of black American judges and African judges, sponsored by a non-profit group, The African Judicial Network. It was the brainchild of Judge Mary Terrell, whom I greatly admire. At the conference, we exchanged ideas about judging, calendar control, and judicial independence. I was invited at the last minute to replace a no-show, but Judge Terrell treated me as if I had been a part of the group since its inception. Many of the judges from Mali, Nigeria, Uganda, and South Africa were from the most respected tribal families, with a long history of colonial education and world travel. They referred to the litigants who appeared before them as peasants and laughed at the ignorance of villagers who wanted to punish their neighbors for lightning strikes. I and four other American judges had been relegated to a native-built hotel near the edge of the city, and from my bathroom window I could see city dwellers emerge at dawn to light fires in the courtyards across the street. They used the heated water for bathing and cooking in the common areas—a dirt-filled circle surrounded by sheds.

None of the screens kept mosquitoes or other bugs from devouring me the first night I stayed at the "hotel from hell." The other judges stayed at the fancy downtown hotel where the meetings were held. Built by Russians, it featured working central air conditioning, a swimming pool, and windows and doors that fit tightly. I called it the palace. I announced (untruthfully) that I and the other judges would return to the United States immediately if we were not allowed to move into the palace.

On our last day at the hotel from hell, four of us waited on the patio to be whisked away to the palace for the remainder of the stay. The hotel employee who had been lounging on a white plastic chair outside the door abandoned his post for the first time. Relieved to be able to sit for what might turn out to be a long wait, I quickly took his place. Under the foam cushion, something long and hard pushed against my hip. I lifted the edge of the cushion and uncovered the wooden handle of a two-foot-long machete. This had been the hotel's security system. I laughed when I lifted the cushion to expose the weapon, but the other judges were not amused.

In Uganda, the United Nations truck and driver had transported me, the police officer, and the soldiers from The White House to the banks of Lake Victoria shortly after dawn. The ferry would take us across the lake, which was so large that the other side was not visible from shore. It was like an ocean, but the bank was covered in six-foot-tall lime-green grasses that swayed in the humid breeze and concealed the ground. The ferry consisted of three-inch-thick planks of wood, each twelve inches across. These planks were lashed together with braided tree branches, and a railing consisting of rusty plumbing pipe ran along two sides of the craft. It was actually a primitive raft with an outboard motor bolted onto one end. The operators collected cash from the first few arrivals, and one of them grabbed an empty gasoline can from shore and trotted down the muddy road. Upon his return about an hour later, he emptied the can into the motor, and I thought we were ready to depart.

We could not depart, however, until the ferry was dangerously overcrowded with more vehicles and passengers. This process of overcrowding took so long that vendors hawking roasted corn on the cob and stewed meat walked among the hungry passengers, hoping for a sale. I thought the pregnant young woman was a vendor. She smiled broadly as she approached the uniformed police officer near our truck, and she clutched a wrinkled, half-filled brown paper bag in her hands. No sale was consummated, however. When I saw them part company, I asked the officer what had transpired. "She want a ride after we cross the lake," the officer said, enigmatically. Concerned about the health of the young woman, I asked, "What did you tell her?" The pleasant officer smiled at me and replied, "I say we got no space left inside the truck." I took the remark from the plump, kind-hearted official to be a polite way of refusing the request, since the open truck bed had to be a torture, even for the hardened soldiers. There were no seats or cushions back there and the metal floor was at least two feet from the ground.

As the ferry began to fill past capacity, I hoped the young woman did not have far to travel. My mind wandered to the speeches that I would give on the other side of Lake Victoria and to the soap and biscuits that we had purchased for the children in the refugee camp. The area surrounding the camp was at the mercy of evil men who had been waging a guerilla war against their own government for years. Small children and frail old men and women were the only civilians alive in the camps now. Everyone else had been killed or kidnapped.

Several hours passed while we waited for the ferry to depart from the shore. Finally, the outboard motor began to sputter. "Hurry, run and get into the truck," I heard the officer shout out. I roused myself from my daydream and raced to the passenger door. I flung the door open and threw myself inside as the truck made for the first available position on the ferry.

An hour later, we reached the other side of Lake Victoria. Night fell as we hurtled down muddy, pitted roads for two more hours. We came to a halt outside a huge prison gate surrounded by a wall.

I recognized the pregnant woman with the paper bag as she waddled away from the truck into the inky night. It was the woman from the ferry who had asked for a ride. "How did she get here?" I asked, mystified. "We give her ride," announced the officer, with pride. "But how?" I asked. I was confused. "You hear me tell her get in the truck," she said patiently. "I thought you were talking to me," I said sheepishly. She shook her head with dismay. "No, I talking to she. The father of she unborn child work in this prison. She travel to see he. We save she life, probably. It take two days walk this far, and she maybe killed or raped on the road walking. She have no money. She happy to ride in the truck with the soldiers. She very grateful to us." I still did not understand. "If she had no money, how would she be able to travel for two days to the prison?" I asked. The officer remained patient with me. "Nobody have money here. Somebody share food and let she sleep in hut maybe." I thought about the jarring ride that I had just experienced as I sat in the cushioned, spacious passenger seat, protected by the windshield and bug spray. How had she even managed to climb onto the open back of the truck? The ruts, stones, and craters would have been unbearable for me in the open metal truck bed, and I was not eight months pregnant. And how would I have survived a two-day walk with a wrinkled paper bag? I had no more questions, because I was rendered speechless, speeding through the Ugandan bush on an unpaved road.

As I sat in the truck, I thought once more about the possibility of danger on the trip, and my mind raced to the last time I had been terrified while traveling. I stood in darkness in the middle of the common area of the small Haitian village, and I repeated the lies in French and English. "We have no more money," I shouted at the gathering crowd. "We spent all our money on this trash in Port-au-Prince. You must take us to the tap tap, so that we can return to Club Med. They are searching for us. We have been missing too long, since early this morning." I roughly snatched large newspaper-wrapped pieces of art from the arms of my girlfriend Dana, and shoved them toward the hostile crowd. Angrily, I offered them my own similarly wrapped pieces, certain that everyone in the village regarded with contempt anyone who spent good money on useless oil paintings and decorative hammered ironwork. We were silly, spoiled Americans who could never understand hunger pangs and hopelessness so profound that they could be transformed into violence in a heartbeat.

Now it was nearly midnight, and we had left the resort in the early morning for our shopping trip in the capital of Haiti. It had taken the entire week to arrange the excursion. On the beach, small boys with brown stick arms and legs sold jewel-colored eight-by-ten-inch oil paintings done on burlap-stretched canvases. The oils were transported in black plastic garbage bags in the hulls of leaky hand-carved, splintery canoes, which they paddled across foot-high ocean waves that threatened to overtake them and their precious cargo. Vendors were forbidden on the beach, but it was impossible to stop the boaters from landing and then relieving sunbathers of their cash in exchange for the art. Dana and I had both read about the Iron Market in our guidebooks, and on the plane we had discussed taking an excursion to visit the site where Africans had been sold into slavery to work the sugarcane plantations that enabled the lucrative rum trade to flourish. A well-organized slave rebellion freed the natives from the French, who were soon forced to sell the Louisiana Purchase lands to the Americans to recoup the loss. But it was the jewel colors on the small canvases sparkling on the beach that finally motivated us to search out the art galleries in Port-au-Prince that had also been described in the guides.

Dana and I had spent the week questioning the tour directors, Club Med personnel, and even a Haitian employee about our plans. To our utter dismay, no tours were scheduled for the city and nobody was willing to accompany us there. "There is only the tap tap, Miss," the travel professional explained. The slender Frenchwoman with the freckled shoulders obviously considered this alternative to be out of the question, and no taxis or no private drivers were available for travel into the city at any price. "The tap tap is an open truck with benches," she explained. "The Haitians sit on them with their chickens and small goats which they take to market. It is very crowded and it costs one American dollar each way for the two of you. You can flag it down in the morning on the road outside the Club Med property, if you prefer." It sounded like the makings of a great Caribbean adventure. I had only one final question for the petite blonde. "Is it safe?" I asked. She raised her head briefly from the magazine she had already begun to read. "Oh, yes," she replied with a dismissive shrug of her perfect right shoulder. "But of course."

Undaunted, Dana and I went back to the pygmy-tribesman-looking Haitian kitchen helper who had described the bustling, sophisticated city to us during the week. "Will you go to the city with us tomorrow?" I asked him as he swept the area around the swimming pool. He looked startled. "We will pay you," I added. He chuckled nervously. "No," he said. "I must work tomorrow. Yesterday was my day off. You will be perfectly safe. The Iron Market is in the center of the city, and everyone knows where it is. Everyone shops there for items they cannot make at home. Farmers also sell grain and vegetables there and it is crowded every day. Just watch out for pickpockets and hide your cash. I bought this watch there." He held up his wrist so that Dana and I could admire the knock-off Movado that did not tell time. The braided metal band gleamed in the harsh sunlight as he scurried away from us, toward the kitchen. Dana and I both agreed that he was probably exaggerating about the cafes and sophisticated night life, but why would he encourage us to venture into a city of danger?

Dana thought she was tough and I did too. She was four inches taller than me and brown-skinned, with gleaming dark hair that fell in ringlets below her slender shoulders. A twenty-inch waist gave way to dramatically rounded hips and thighs. All men adored her and many whistled at her and called out to her whenever she wore clothes that revealed her voluptuous figure. Her bright, almond-shaped eyes often crinkled in a mysterious smile and her wide mouth above a square jaw and pointy chin often opened to let laughter escape. Dana was a funny, smart attorney whom I had met on the Hill and her sweet, flexible nature made her an ideal traveling companion. She was also a prosecutor, a job for a tough cookie.

The Club Med trip was an ideal getaway for both of us. Shortly after our arrival, I had taken as a lover the Club Med beach manager. He stood about six-and-a-half feet tall and he had the sleek muscles of a professional diver, which he was. An ebony-hued native of Barbados, he taught me to dance to reggae music and then sat and watched me dance alone until two AM each night at the resort's disco. "Dance for me, girl," he whispered. He was too exhausted to dance after working twelve hours on the beach, but he was not too exhausted to sneak me into his cramped Club Med employee hovel, where we made frenetic love all night. I loved everything about him, from his closely shaved head to his scarred fingers and his musical, Caribbean accent.

He regaled me with stories about the European women guests and his sexual exploits with them, and I regaled him with my body. Unfortunately, despite my pleas, Dana had refused to share him or to take my place in his narrow bed. "You don't know what you're missing," I pleaded with her. "He is a treasure to be shared by the entirety of womankind. He is perfect in every way, and his penis is in proportion to his height!" Of course, I also would have enjoyed watching the two most beautiful people at the resort making love, but it was not to be.

After breakfast, Dana and I smiled conspiratorially as we walked away from the resort to wave down a tap tap. We left behind us a twelve-foot-high, two-foot-thick brick wall where a guard, who was armed with an automatic machine gun and a portable radio, sat in a gatehouse. He protected the resort, a sprawling Shangri-La of a place, with manicured lawns, flowering shrubs, pristine beaches, and stucco guest houses. Like most Caribbean resorts, it had probably first been created by slaves, who transformed it from a dense jungle to a sugarcane plantation, where the Carib Indians and African natives were enslaved for centuries. We would miss the French cuisine and fine wine that would be served for lunch, but we were looking forward to our adventure. We had both dressed carefully for the occasion, avoiding jewelry and clothing that might identify us as American. I had seen light-skinned Haitian women in newspapers and magazine articles, and I thought I could blend in. Both of Dana's parents had been born in the Islands and, although she was a brown-skinned American through and through, we both thought she looked like an Island girl.

As soon as we passed the guard post, Haiti changed. Every footstep scattered puffs of dirt and the area was denuded of trees, shrubbery, and vegetation. It looked like Mars. All of it had been used for fuel or food. A glance to the right revealed a ragged woman stooping over a narrow stream of water that ran like a sewer through the dust. She was scrubbing a piece of tattered clothing without using soap. Her long skirt was also in tatters, her slender feet were bare, and she wore a ragged kerchief Aunt Jemima style over her uneven bush-style hair. Her smile in response to our waves revealed four missing front teeth. She could have been any age between twenty and fifty. It was impossible to tell from her bony face and shrunken torso.

To the left was an empty, arid road as far as the eye could see. We let three vans pass us by before we concluded during the hour-long wait that they were tap taps. When the next one arrived, we waved our arms frantically and the driver came to a screeching halt. We scurried aboard and the vehicle accelerated like a rocket. I addressed the young male driver in French and English. "We want to go to the Iron Market in Port-au-Prince," I said. "How much is the fare?" He looked at me blankly. I held up one American dollar and Dana did the same. As we attempted to hand him the money, the entire van erupted. All the seats were occupied by small goats and chickens and scrawny Haitians who were dressed in homemade clothes that had long been reduced to rags. Their faces were all the exact same color, a bluish black that I had seen only in *National Geographic* magazine stories about obscure African bush tribes. All the passengers had the same coppery orange hair color, the result of malnutrition, which also caused the gaunt limbs and tiny paunches that each possessed. Most were barefoot, with stone-hard soles exposed. We were not blending in. It took me a while to comprehend the cause of the spontaneous eruption. "Tourists pay five dollars U.S. for each person," they shouted in unison in heavily accented French. Everyone was demanding that the driver charge us extra. We were confronted by people who spoke neither English nor French and who understood neither language when we spoke to them. I meekly handed the driver two five-dollar bills and we sat in the van, which took on more passengers and animals until we were overloaded as we sped toward the capital city, over an hour away. I could feel Dana trembling slightly as she was shoved against me by the growing crowd.

The driver ordered the two of us out of the van as soon as we reached the city. "Get out," he shouted. "Get out, now! Go! Go!" We were the only passengers left. When I asked "Where is the Iron Market?" in French and English, he scowled and slammed the door in my face. We turned away from the departing van and found ourselves on a paved sidewalk, surrounded by a river of people who looked exactly like our departing fellow passengers. This was not good. In a daze, the two of us walked toward the most dense section of the city, away from the road we had just left. There were no street signs or traffic lights. Four-wheel-drive vehicles, driven by Europeans who stared straight ahead like zombies, careened past us. By the time we had traveled three blocks, we had acquired a retinue of street children who demanded money for pebbles and pieces of paper trash, or gaping wounds that they were anxious to display to us. Our hellish walk came to an end when we spotted a military garrison in the next block. It was a two-story building surrounded by well-fed Haitian men who wore combat boots, camouflage uniforms, ugly scowls, and automatic machine guns. We smiled at our rescuers. I walked up to the nearest one and asked in English and French, "Where is the Iron Market?" He barked something out in a patois that I could not get. When I asked the question again, slower, he pointed vaguely to his left with the barrel of his weapon. We dutifully walked to his left for four more blocks. This time we acquired a new following of scrawny adult men, grinning vendors who offered us wood carvings of grotesque male genitals.

When we spotted a dusty hardware store, we ran toward it. Inside, a stout, balding middle-aged European male spoke English with a thick French accent. "The Iron Market is ten blocks in that direction," he said, pointing in the opposite direction. "Yes, there is beautiful ironwork there. The Haitians use discarded oil barrels for it. They cut them and hammer them into lovely works of art, and nobody does it better. There is also a street not far from the market where gallery owners will sell you gorgeous oils for almost nothing." He wanted us to linger but we were on a mission and it was getting late. We had already missed lunch, and we did not want to be late for dinner at the resort.

A fourteen-block walk brought us to the Iron Market, which dominated the middle of the city. An ornate brick wall supported decorative panels of thick iron that were bent into complex swirls. It was six square blocks of an open-air market wrapped up in black lace and it was beautiful, in spite of its history of genocide and evil. The ornate sections of iron had several openings leading onto the sidewalks and a huge flared roof provided shade from the merciless sun and from tropical storms. Inside the low walls, women sold wares from mounds of homemade clothing, metal cooking pots, and bushels of grain. Dana and I were the only tourists in the market, and we were petrified. But we had reached our objective, and we would not be denied. It did not take us long to find the ironwork vendors and we soon purchased as much as we could carry back to the resort for the trip home.

When we emerged from the Iron Market, we were assailed once again by beggars and peddlers, and we could not find any art galleries in the area. Suddenly, Gabriel emerged. The adolescent boy was dressed in tennis shoes, jeans, and a clean tee shirt. He was Dana's height, lighter-skinned than the population around him, and he spoke halting English. After agreeing to be our guide, we followed him for six blocks as he set out at a brisk pace for "the best art gallery in town." Indeed, the gallery was amazing. It was owned by a man who could have been the younger brother of the hardware store proprietor. Brilliant canvases, framed in splintery wood, were piled waist-high on the floor all around us, stacked against the walls, and leaning precariously so that every inch of the interior was covered with them. We were in Haitian oil-painting heaven. Dana and I soon emerged from the gallery with rolls of canvas to stuff in our suitcases. We were also starving.

Our guide had waited for us on the sidewalk, where he continued to slap beggars and vendors when they got too close to us. We were headed to "the best restaurant in town" for a late lunch. The meal turned out to be classic French cuisine in a fancy restaurant where we were the only diners. Five waiters and two managers watched us eat, and Gabriel refused to consume any food or drink any beverages. Instead, he sat across from us and kept up a steady stream of questions about the United States, the country that obsessed him. Dana and I relaxed in the fine restaurant for the first time since our departure in the morning, but it was time to take the tap tap back. I realized that our guide and most of the Haitians we had encountered were illiterate. Instead of giving merely the address and title of Club Med Resort as our destination, I brandished the unique Club Med logo on our identification cards to indicate to Gabriel where we wanted to go. He nodded his head and walked us about ten blocks to a group of vans that were headed out of the city in the dusk.

When our guide left us, he had tears in his eyes and he refused to take any money from us. I took my Walt Disney cap off my head and jammed it onto his. That made him smile and he waved goodbye. I showed the surly tap tap driver the Club Med logo on the card, and I asked him in English and in French whether he would take us to Club Med. "We want to go to Club Med," I said. "Is this the right tap tap?" He nodded in agreement and I paid him the cash he demanded. We joined the passengers in the van but the vehicle pulled away from the curb only when it was filled beyond its capacity with Haitians, their wares, and their live animals—a process that took about an hour. The van took off at breakneck speed and, two hours later, the driver stopped the van abruptly and ordered us in French to leave the van. We were in the middle of a small village and I refused to budge. "This is not Club Med," I shouted angrily. "Take us to Club Med, now!" When the driver approached us to shove Dana from the van, I stepped out. She followed, and he slammed the door on us. We were abandoned. The night was moonless and pure ink as a crowd gathered quickly. The village had no electricity. It was constructed of mud and corrugated tin. There was one kerosene lamp.

Four men strode confidently toward us and I displayed the identification card. "Take me to Club Med," I insisted in French and English. The closest male spoke for the group. "Give me your money," he said in plain English. He looked exactly like Jack Johnson, the heavyweight boxer, except he was darker. Then he pointed dramatically at the small purses that Dana and I still carried on our shoulders. The crowd grew

201

larger and all the villagers drew closer, so that they could see and hear better. I was angry when I heard the demand, but I was not surprised. Why else had we been transported to this God-forsaken place? Surely the tap tap driver did not think that we lived in one of the tilted wooden or mud huts that we could see dimly beyond the crowd. When I looked up into the eyes of the robber, he could tell that I was angry. In a flash, I was in the grip of an awful rage. I was angry that human beings had been sold into slavery at the Iron Market that we had just seen, angry that their progeny lived with hunger and filth in a beautiful country decimated by violence and greed, and angry that the man in front of me had been so driven to attempt desperate acts of violence himself.

As I shoved the precious objects of art at the crowd, and lied to them about the cash we had left, I hoped that we would be spared. The robber demanded money again. "Give me all your money, now!" he shouted in a louder, more menacing tone. Now it was my turn to yell hysterically. "We *have* no more money!" I screamed crazily in English and French, feigning some kind of psychotic breakdown for the villagers. "I *told* you! The people at Club Med are looking for us, because we are very late. We spent all our money on this Haitian trash. Where is the tap tap?" Standing mute beside me, Dana held my hand and shook so violently I could hear her teeth chattering. In the middle of my third tirade, the robber turned his back on me in disgust. He began a muttered conversation in patois with the tough gang members who surrounded him. On my right, I spied an elderly, stooped little man approaching Dana. "I will take you to the tap tap," he whispered in French. "Follow me, quickly." Then, he disappeared into the gloom. What choice did we have? Dana and I scurried behind him into nothingness. After trotting for about half a mile, the old man halted and pointed in the distance to a vehicle idling in the dark. I pressed two U.S. bills of some denomination into his bony hand, and Dana and I hopped onto the tap tap. I gave the sullen driver two crumpled, sweat-soaked twenty-dollar bills and showed him the Club Med decal. I pointed at it. "Do you know where Club Med is?" I asked in French and English. "Will you take us there right now?" The driver nodded yes to both questions and did not even wait to fill the truck with passengers. In two hours, we were back in Port-au-Prince, near the deserted Iron Market. An hour after that, we were at the Club Med guard shack. The first tap tap had taken us in the opposite direction, to leave us at the robbers' village.

Dana was still shaking violently when we walked up to the guard post. The guard cradled his machine gun as if it were an infant while he examined our identification wrist badges. "Can we get something to eat from the kitchen?" I asked in French. "No," he replied. "Can we get a soda or something to drink from anywhere?" "No," he replied. He waved us into the compound with a gesture of profound boredom. "The kitchen is closed," he said. "It is three AM." Dana and I were exhausted and still traumatized, but I had one more task to perform before we left the immediate area. "Wait a minute," I shouted. "I told you on the way back that I would do this if we got here alive, and I am a woman of my word!" I dropped all my parcels on the grass, knelt down, and spread my palms out on the ground. Then I kissed the ground with a loud smack. Dana and I both smiled as we walked away from the thick wall. The guard shook his head in disgust at the two foolish American women.

# Scene Twenty-Eight
## Something Special

He sat at the table between me and his wife and tried to make sense of what had happened two hours earlier, when he woke up at the castle. Joe was a stocky, Erroll Flynn type and his wife, Maria, was a brunette Lucille Ball, but with larger breasts. Her face was set in a frown and she had not said a word since the server had placed breakfast on the table. "I was sleepy and confused," he said. "When I touched you, I thought I was touching Maria. And when I got inside you, it was amazing. You felt just like her and you moved just like her too—on the inside, I mean." Bewildered, Joe looked at me and then at his wife. He expected one of us to answer his unspoken question: "How could this have happened?"

I knew exactly how it had happened. I took a bite from the stack of blueberry pancakes in front of me and I sipped the jasmine tea with lemon and fake sugar. It started in Paradise Island, a year before the morning in the castle. I had spent a long weekend in Club Med, where I had met Paul, a pony-tailed, middle-aged Steven Seagal type. He was there with his wife Laura, who reminded me of a blonde buxom Pamela Anderson, and their two children, Adam and Eve. I was there with my teen-aged daughter, Mitch. When Paul began to flirt shamelessly with me in front of his mute, staring wife, I did not tell him that I had recognized them from an old swinger magazine that featured soft porn. It had shown both of them at a party in various stages of undress and sexy poses.

By the end of the stay on Paradise Island, I had exchanged addresses and telephone numbers with the couple and I had also promised to let them know when I would be in California, where they owned a house that was actually a castle. A drawing of it adorned Paul's business card. The drawing clearly depicted a moat and turrets, but Paul also described a fancy gazebo and several caves, all of which had been constructed in the Hollywood Hills by the same engineers who had created Disneyland.

The couple often rented out the property as a movie set. Although my skepticism was at war with my curiosity, I had accepted Paul's invitation to "come and see us and spend the night" the next time I was in California. He also promised to arrange "something special" for me if I decided to accept the invitation. He had confided that he and his wife had been swingers for several years and said that they were both looking forward to a visit from me at my earliest convenience.

My earliest convenience was a year later, when I visited my girlfriend Myra in Los Angeles for two weeks. Paul sent a car and driver for me, and we headed for the Hollywood Hills, which turned out to be mountains with canyons, hairpin turns, and an impenetrable forest. The car came to a halt in front of an ancient-looking castle, complete with moat, drawbridge, turrets, and towers. The opening to a mock cave yawned nearby. The twenty-foot-tall wooden door of the castle creaked open to reveal an immense hallway with a full set of decorated armor that was illuminated by a circular candelabra, from which Errol Flynn might have swung. The "something special" for me was not only Paul's lovely wife but, also, an additional couple—Joe and Maria.

After a hurried supper and a few glasses of wine, all five of us repaired to the main bedroom. I had seen it filmed in several porn movies. The huge, round, custom-made bed was covered with a wine-red velvet spread and the ceiling consisted of a circular mirror that perfectly reflected candles and naked flesh. When viewed from a prone position, it flared out from central wooden beams like spokes from a giant wheel. Paul's wife lay down in a seductive pose, vulnerable in total nudity. She was a Marilyn Monroe look-alike. Only one thing marred the picture she presented: Her face was a rigid mask of fear. I wondered how long it had been since she had experienced an orgasm. I looked at Paul, who was reading my mind.

Paul pointed gracefully at his wife as she watched me. "Please," he whispered to me. In a pose strangely like one done by Marilyn, she covered her breasts with one arm. I knew what that meant: Her breasts were off-limits. I looked over at Paul again. "Please," he whispered again. That did the trick, as I do love a challenge. I used my tongue, teeth, nose, chin, forehead, fingers, and entire body to bring Laura as much pleasure as I could. Meanwhile, Paul, Joe, and Maria were engaged in various couplings and sucking combinations. Many of their activities involved parts of my anatomy that were not presently being used for pleasuring Laura. "Maria, don't you want to do Lillian?" I heard Joe say at some point. "She is so beautiful." "No," came the whispered response. "There is too much hair down there." I giggled and made a mental note to get a trim in the near future.

It took me about three hours to pleasure Laura to my utmost ability. During that entire time, I had not touched her enormous breasts once, but she had silently and persistently massaged and sucked her own breasts constantly. Twice I felt her body shudder and three times I heard her gasp. Were these orgasms? By the end of the session with her, I was exhausted from my own nuclear-powered orgasms and from my contortions with Laura. Surrounded from head to toe with sweaty, human flesh, I fell into a near coma. I was in Lillian heaven.

Sometime after dawn, a hunk of the human flesh penetrated me. I had my back to him, and he held me tightly. He shouted, "Oh Maria," as he ejaculated against my cervix. I moaned, "Uh, oh," as I came twice. When Joe finally opened his eyes, he realized that he had made some kind of mistake, and he immediately began to babble about breakfast. When I opened my eyes, I saw Paul standing motionless across the room, staring out of a narrow castle window. I picked up some of my clothing and walked in his direction. He turned to me and I saw something close to awe and admiration in his face. He pointed to the beautiful Laura, still sleeping in a charming fetal position. "She never experienced an orgasm until last night," he said quietly. "Thank you." I just smiled and looked out the window.

I dressed quickly, and so did Joe and his wife. I slept in the back seat during the ride down the mountain. We walked into the first restaurant we encountered in Los Angeles, and the babbling continued after we ordered breakfast. He said, "Why was it that I could not tell the difference?" Joe was still upset. I took another bite of the blueberry pancakes. I was ravenous, and he needed to vent in a public place so that they would not hurt each other. "When did you realize that I was not Maria?" I asked. I already knew the answer and my mind began to wander again. I knew how this could have happened. It had happened before.

It happened in Amsterdam, five years earlier. A girlfriend, Debbie, lived and worked in Europe and I visited her every few months. Over the course of several visits, I had come to know Debbie's best friend there, Edie, very well. A native Australian, Edie had lived and worked in England for several years. Edie and I both agreed that we were nearly identical where it really counted—our worldview, taste in men, sense of humor, and temperament. This affinity was scary, not only because we were different races and grew up in different parts of the world, but because we were really different physically. Edie is nearly six-feet tall, with platinum blonde hair, big blue eyes, milky skin marbled with blue veins, and a face like Marlene Dietrich. In physical stature, I am closer to Debbie. We wear the same dress, shoe, hat, glove, and coat sizes and we even have the same eyeglass prescription.

The three of us traveled to Amsterdam for a weekend of adventure. Since it was my first visit, our first stop was a bar in the middle of town. It was filled with typical Amsterdam men— all nearly six-and-a-half feet tall with giant shoulders, blonde hair, and square jaws. My problem in the bar was that I was so much shorter than the other customers that they could not see me in the crowd. I was being jostled and bruised by elbows, hips, feet, and shoulders. After a half an hour, I could not take it any longer. I shouted to the two women that I would meet them on the sidewalk outside. There, I engaged in one of my favorite activities—people watching and imagining stories about them.

An old city riddled with canals, Amsterdam is the Venice of the north. I watched people getting on and off houseboats, dinner boats, ferries, and row boats. The city is filled with bicycle riders and I watched people peddling, sitting on handlebars while someone else peddled, and nearly getting run over by every variety of rusty cycle known to mankind. Most importantly, I watched people smoking weed, which is not really legal in Amsterdam but everybody does it. In about an hour, Debbie and Edie emerged from the bar with a beautiful man in tow, a young version of Peter O'Toole. His name was Francis, and he was happy to escort us to the marijuana café—where they rolled joints for you—to the porn movie theater, to the red-light district, and to the disco run by a cult. Best of all, he spoke English. Edie spent the night on the houseboat that Francis had docked in a canal, and Debbie and I went back to the hotel, a private home so old that the entire building was canted askew and the floor sloped like a cartoon structure. The next day, Edie met us at the hotel filled with news of Francis.

Francis was a considerate, enthusiastic, well-endowed lover. She was crazy about him and wanted to share him with us. He was a treasure to be experienced by all of womankind, and we really should not miss the opportunity. The three of us had dinner together and people-watched at an outdoor café, and we agreed to meet Edie's new lover at the hotel later. True to her word, Edie showed up a few hours later with Francis in tow. He was everything Edie had described, but Debbie begged off. I joined Edie and Francis as soon as I got a good look at the curly blonde mane of hair that covered his entire chest. I could not wait to get my hands and teeth in it. The room had blackout shades from World War II and, as soon as we clicked the lamps off, we were plunged into impenetrable darkness.

I found myself unable to distinguish between the two bodies by feel, even though they were different genders. I could hardly tell whether I was touching my own arm or someone else's. It was unique and exquisitely sensual, and I was not the only one who felt that way. After a couple of hours of strenuous sexual activity, Francis began to babble. "I cannot tell the difference," he moaned. "This is so wonderful! There are two beautiful women here in the bed with me and I cannot tell the difference. Oh my God, I'm coming again!"

Joe wanted to ask me a question and my mind snapped back to the breakfast table in Los Angeles. "Lillian, I answered your question, but you did not answer mine," he said. "When I held you and made love to you, why was it that I could not tell the difference between you and Maria?" They were waiting for me to give them an answer that made sense. Maria stared at her uneaten food. If I did not give him an answer, he would start whining again. "Maria and I are the same complexion and we have the same body type," I said. "And I had my back turned to you. Let's go." I stood up and walked out of the restaurant. I was bored, and I had finished eating the blueberry pancakes.

# Scene Twenty-Nine
## Fella and Samson

It was my fault. I was a terrible dog owner. I had nobody to blame but myself. I should not have left Fella tied to the garden railing for such a long time, but I had gotten distracted by the book I was reading and I had forgotten that the dog existed, even though I had taken in the adorable tan and white Lhasa Apso more than two years earlier. He could not have unfastened the knot himself, so somebody had stolen him and I thought I knew who had done it. Across the street from my complex is Greenleaf Gardens, public housing that is a warren of townhouses and apartment buildings. I was convinced that Fella had been taken by residents of the public housing complex but, first, I would go to the small playground that we used as a dog park and make inquiries. It was a warm, sunny day in May and maybe one of the dog owners had spotted my dog in the company of some stranger.

Sure enough, Jacki sat hunched over her smoldering cigarette while her obese Chihuahua, Chocolate, investigated the shrubbery. She was my favorite neighbor, because she was friendly, talkative, and funny. As usual, she wore her hair pulled back in a severe ponytail. She was the exact color of her dog. Although she was in her forties, she wore a trendy black sweater and matching skintight stretch pants. "Fella is  missing," I called out. "Have you seen him around?  I think somebody untied him from the railing outside my house." Her smile turned abruptly into a frown. "No, I haven't seen him, but don't worry," she responded quickly. "We are talking about Fella, now.  Whoever took him will bring him back soon. You'll see."

I could not decide whether to be amused, comforted, or offended by the remark, so I mumbled something to Jacki and continued my search of the neighborhood. Sure, I thought, Fella may be a little quirky. My niece, Kim, had  persuaded me to take him in. Hungry and abandoned without a collar, he had followed her and her two children home in the Anacostia section of town. She had called me because she knew that I was looking for a replacement for my mother's dog—a mangy, hyper brown Chihuahua who barked in my face and pooped on the carpet whenever I visited her. I had not allowed her to bring the animal when she moved into my house. Her dementia had caused her to fixate on his absence and I thought a replacement pet would ease the transition to her new living arrangement. The vet estimated Fella's age to be two years, determined that he was a Lhasa Apso, and opined that he had been abandoned and living on the streets for two weeks when I brought him in for shots and an examination. After being bathed and groomed, he looked like a totally different animal.

Unfortunately, Fella and my mother were not a good match. Abused as a puppy, he refused to sit in her lap or to allow her to pick him up from the floor. My mother was ashamed to admit that she could not feed herself, due to her advanced dementia, and the dog was happy to gobble up the food that she surreptitiously dropped to the floor. Soon, the animal tracked the food all over the house—after stepping in it—and he had to be locked out of her room at meal times. He was not happy about being locked out of any room in the house, and he barked to show his displeasure. My mother died a few months after I acquired Fella. I had him neutered, returned him to Kim, and forgot about him.

When I visited Kim less than two weeks later, I was shocked at the transformation Fella had undergone. His perfectly groomed fur was tangled and matted. He had bug bites all over his exposed skin and he had scratched them bloody. His surgery site was obviously infected and he was in pain as he watched me with giant marble-brown eyes. I thought about the dozens of animals that my family had neglected and abused in our crowded childhood home. The list included a monkey, gerbils, parakeets, rabbits, turtles, baby chicks, cats, and dogs. My mother had acquired all of them from boyfriends on a whim and she disposed of them in the same fashion. I always knew that was cruel and I could not abandon Fella to the whims of my niece. I took him back to the vet and Fella became my first dog.

Fella had a few quirks, but anyone would want to keep him. He growled when anyone tried to pick him up, and he refused to sit on anyone's lap. When I got him, he ran away at every opportunity. Outside of my house, he tried to urinate every five minutes. After reading many books on dog training—and much trial and error—I trained him to be walked, to remain seated on the interior stairs when I left the house without him, and to use a poop pad in the house in an emergency. Outside of my house, Fella did his business anywhere that smelled appropriate to him. A dirty carpet or stairway was fair game. He still refuses to allow anyone else to pick him up, but he sits in any lap if it's in a moving vehicle. Worst of all, Fella is fearless. He chases horses, large dogs, ducks, and pigeons with equal abandon. He is quite a character, but he is *my* character.

As I marched toward Greenleaf Gardens, I was determined to confront anyone who took Fella, and I would demand his return, but I also began to steel myself for the possibility that I might never see him again. Maybe I could adjust, like I had adjusted to the absence of Samson, the grey New England coon cat who had been my first pet. I was twenty-four years old, married, and living with my husband in an apartment on Fort Totten Drive in Northeast when I first saw the cat. "Can Walter come out?" a group of small children wanted to know when I answered the knock on the door. I recognized them from the neighborhood. My husband, clueless and childish, was their favorite adult, and I had no idea what he did with them to inspire such devotion. "Sure, I'll get him," I replied. Walter soon disappeared with the knot of ten-year-olds down the hall somewhere. I returned to my reading and forgot about him and the children.

A couple of hours later, Walter returned with an armful of what looked like grey dust. It was a cat, who had been trapped in the exhaust hose of a clothes dryer downstairs. The kids had persuaded Walter to rescue him. He was a gaunt, weak animal with long hair that swept the floor and a tail that was at least twelve inches long, hanging down like a mop from Walter's arm. His huge black eyes were surrounded by colors that made him appear to wear a mask over his upper face. The cat looked at me and it was love at first sight. He let me bathe him, trim thorns from his underbelly, and brush him. He sat in my lap and slept at the foot of our bed at night. He was my cat. I named him Samson, from the Bible, because of his huge fur.

Seven years later, when we bought the townhouse, Samson became an outdoor cat. He brought me birds that he had stalked patiently and killed, even after I put a bell around his neck and even though he had been neutered years earlier. I cleaned the wounds that he acquired from his battles with the neighborhood cats and dogs. Unable to adjust to the baby, his biggest rival, Samson had watched her from dark corners, and he circled her warily. By the time she could crawl, the two of them started a game that would not end well. He walked toward her slowly. Intentionally twitching his fluffy tail to get her attention, he kept his tail just out of her reach. She grabbed at the tail with a chubby fist and squealed in toothless ecstasy when he snatched it out of her grasp. I intervened when I could, but they were both too fast for me. I could not prevent the cat from teasing her with his tail, and I could not stop her from scurrying across the oak floor behind him. One day, the inevitable happened.

Mitch was eleven months old when she finally grabbed Samson's tail in a grubby, tight fist. She howled in fiendish delight at her good luck. I watched helplessly as Samson whirled around and silently raked his right-front paw across her face, from her forehead down to her chin, just missing her eyes. The claws that he kept sharpened on neighborhood trees left trails of blood that dripped onto her green lace bib. She released the tail and howled like an animal. While she bawled, I tried to kill the cat with a mop, a broom, and my bare hands, but he was much too fast, and I was unable to land a single blow. Finally, I opened the back door and Samson ran through it in a streak of grey. I never saw him again. Mitch's wounds healed without a trace of a scar.

I had been able to adjust to the loss of Samson, but that was different. After all, I had tried to kill him, and he had acted out of jealousy. I would never be able to get over Fella's loss. The anger would be too great. My anger was obvious to the knots of shirtless drug sellers with six-pack abs who stood around across the street. They watched silently as I peered into the doors and windows of the two-story houses, and they did not challenge me when I got close enough to search the backyards and the areas around the clotheslines. There was no point in asking whether they had seen the dog. I knew what the answer would be. By the time I circled the area again, I knew that I would be unable to find him, and I was attracting too much attention. An hour had passed since his disappearance, and Fella was probably already in a speeding car on his way to a new neighborhood. He loved to be taken for a walk and would be happy to allow anyone to untie him from the railing. Friendly to all strangers, he allowed children to poke their fingers in his marble eyes and grab his black gumdrop nose without even growling at them. His love of traveling in a vehicle would allow him to be placed easily in anything with four wheels, without even a bark.

By the time I returned to my block, I had accepted the inevitable, and I bowed my head to fate. But, when I looked up, I saw Fella—tied to the exact spot where I had left him. I asked him what had happened and he just looked at me, patiently waiting to be untied and led to a new adventure. A half-hour later, a group of friendly neighborhood children knocked on my door. They told a fantastic story of encountering Fella as he was being abducted by a gang from Greenleaf Gardens and persuading the gang to let him go, then taking Fella to their building across the street, where he urinated on the floor. They finally remembered where he lived and they tied him up to the railing when nobody came to the door a few minutes ago. They came back to make sure he was okay. When they got to the part about urinating in the apartment building, I remembered Jacki's prediction that he would be returned soon. I laughed, hugged the kids for "rescuing" my dog, and took them all to McDonald's.

# Scene Thirty
## Swimming

"Let's race," he shouted, hopping from one foot to the other at the edge of the swimming pool. I did not know the name of the scrawny little ten-year-old, but I hated him. How did I let the kid talk me into this predicament? I was in ten feet of water on a sunny day, surrounded by six prepubescent boys. This was my idea of hell. I had spent the weekend at Clarence's apartment and his son was bored to tears. Clarence was in his usual foul mood. He was polishing a speech that he was scheduled to deliver in some small town in Iowa. His campaign obligations were staggering because he found it impossible to say no to his Republican benefactors. They liked him and they were confident that he could convince moderate Republicans to support their ultra-conservative agenda and candidates.

As chairman of the EEOC, Clarence's positions on a variety of issues—from abortion rights to affirmative action—were important to the party base although, years before, his party had written off the black vote. I believed the rumors that Clarence would be rewarded with a federal judgeship if he campaigned effectively. I also believed that eventually he would be considered for the Supreme Court to replace the ailing Justice Marshall. Clarence believed it too. Now, in every speech, Clarence had to prove that he could be trusted to remain loyal to the Republican conservative agenda even *after* his appointment to the Supreme Court bench. He had to transform himself into the Republican Party's definition of a true believer. This was no mean feat. No wonder he was in a bad mood. Today, I felt sorry for him and his son.

I went swimming to make twelve-year-old Jamal happy, but I really hated most swimming pools. The chlorine made my eyes sting and get bloodshot, and goggles gave me a headache. When I agreed to accompany Jamal to the pool, I had no idea that I would be the only adult surrounded by a group of sugar-addled miniature, hyper males. My favorite thing to do in the water was to swim lazily on my back, with sunglasses protecting my cornea, while daydreaming about the last tropical island I had visited. The second was snorkeling, sucking air through a tube while I admired Technicolor fish and fantastic coral formations. Right now, I was doing neither. But I was swimming on my back in nine feet of water.

A half-dozen gangly, uncoordinated boys jumped simultaneously into the small pool. "Yay! Let's race!" they shouted, rocketing me to the bottom of the deep area. I relived my last unpleasant encounter with a swimming pool as I fought to reach the surface. I was studying for the D.C. Bar examination so that I could get a license to practice as an assistant United States attorney. In law school, I had to abandon my karate classes because I needed the time to study but, when I graduated and began studying for the Bar, I knew I had to get regular exercise to do my best on the test. I chose swimming classes at the YWCA because they were cheap, convenient, and might save my life one day. I was not a natural swimmer.

For six weeks, I faithfully attended swimming classes, which were taught by an instructor who never entered the water. She stood on the side of the pool and mimed strokes and barked orders to put us through our paces. By the end of the course, I had mastered all the beginner strokes except the crawl, the stroke in which the swimmer is on their stomach with their face in the water. I could not coordinate the breathing with the arm and leg movements. Besides, I wondered, why would anyone want to keep their face down in the nasty chlorine-laced water if they had a choice? I always did the stroke with my eyes closed, and I still was not afraid of the water. Graduation day arrived for the swimmers and the Bar exam was set for the very next day. When we gathered for the graduation swim, the instructor announced that we could not get a certificate unless we could swim the entire length of the pool doing the crawl—swimming on our stomachs. But, in our practices, I had never swum that far using the stroke, because I hated the chlorine so much. I figured that I would just keep my eyes closed and I would be fine.

The swimmers who went before me were great, and they all passed. I figured that it was a piece of cake. When it was my turn, I entered in the shallow end and swam for the deep end, just like they did. I took a breath early on and swam quickly toward the wall. I figured I must have reached it but, when I stretched to grab for the tile, I found only water in front of me. I panicked. I decided to come up for air, but I swallowed a big gulp of water instead. Where was the bottom of the pool? Where was the side of the pool? I swam for the side of the pool to haul myself out and I swallowed more water. Then I heard someone yelling so loud that it penetrated the adrenaline rush of my panic state. The instructor was standing on the side of the pool—three feet from me—and she was shouting at me for all she was worth. "Open your eyes! Open your eyes," she screamed. I had entered the pool with my eyes shut. I'd forgotten to open them and forgotten to turn my head to breathe, so I was swimming blind, in circles in the deep end, with my face in the water. When I opened my eyes, I saw a white pole stretched out into the water, right beside me. "Grab the pole," she screamed. "Grab the pole!" I grabbed the pole and she hauled me out of the water. "You were swimming at a forty-five-degree angle in the deep end with your eyes closed," she explained as I toweled off. The other students looked away, embarrassed for me. All I could think was, "If I can't pass a simple swimming test, how the hell am I going to pass the D.C. Bar exam?"

Surrounded by the ten-year-olds in the pool, I fought my way to the ladder and climbed out of the water. I called out to Jamal to leave the pool, too. We would be late for lunch and Clarence would be in a terrible mood. Jamal climbed out of the water and walked toward me, followed by every boy in the pool. As if they were dazed, they all walked toward me. It was like a scene from *Night of the Living Dead*. They were speechless and their mouths hung open as they stared at me. Wait, I realized, they were all staring at my chest. I looked down. The dunking and my panicky exit had taken their toll on my swimsuit.

The top had given way to the force of the water and both of my breasts had exploded over the edge of the fabric. When I looked down, I saw two pink nipples staring at me and the boys. As everyone gaped, I hurriedly adjusted the suit. In slow motion, the boys turned away and went back to playing. Jamal and I ran to have lunch with his father and we never spoke of the swimsuit incident.

"But why?" Clarence asked, staring at me over his untouched bowl of chicken soup. I said nothing. He began to crush his lips together in a wide crease. "Why are you doing this to me?" He had raised his voice an octave and a silver-haired white couple a few tables away interrupted their silent meal to stare in our direction. Maybe this was not such a good idea. Determined to end my relationship with Clarence, I had chosen a small, dingy Greek restaurant on Capitol Hill for the conversation. I was a regular and my plan was twofold—to minimize the chance of a dramatic scene and to make sure that I did not change my mind. We were seated at my favorite table, in a corner, far from the entrance. If I spoke calmly, Clarence would lower his voice and accept my decision. After all, he must have had some inkling that we had reached this point. It might even be a relief to him.

"It's just not working," I whispered into his bowl. By that, I meant our relationship. Everything else in his life was working just fine. Anita Hill had been a major problem. His buddy, Gil Hardy, had persuaded Clarence to hire her at the Department of Education when he left Senator Danforth's office. She had remained close to Gil when she followed Clarence to the EEOC, where she destroyed morale in the office. Clarence's loyalty to his best friend had prevented him from firing Hill, but Clarence had solved the problem by subsequently finding her a teaching job outside the city, where she would be unable to harm him. He still took her phone calls and catered to her wishes from afar.

His financial problems appeared to be resolved. When I first met him, he had tax problems and big debts. His Spartan lifestyle and obsessive budgeting were defeated by his commitment to educate his son in private schools and his desire to rid himself of a marriage that was not happy. Without my asking for the money, he had repaid the loan I made to him and the passage of time had brought some resolution of his family situation. After his grandfather's death, Clarence rarely mentioned him. The rants stemming from his abandonment by his parents and cruelty by his grandfather no longer generated heart-wrenching sobs and hours of complaint. He no longer dwelled on these matters. Obtaining custody of his son had brought relative peace to Clarence's life. He no longer engaged in protracted arguments with the child's mother about his conduct. Those arguments, however, had been replaced by short monologues which Clarence delivered directly to Jamal. The two-bedroom apartment, with the kitchen and living room between the sleeping areas, allowed father and son to take breaks from each other.

Clarence had taken control of his alcohol abuse. For the past few months, he had refused to consume any alcohol or to serve any in his apartment. Finally, his career was in a good place. Credible rumors were flying that he would soon be appointed to the federal bench and that the Supreme Court was in his near future. Clarence pretended not to believe them but he campaigned tirelessly, maintaining close ties to the Republican crowd and talking to favored reporters until the wee hours of the morning. On his way up in the world of Republicans, Clarence was no longer the raging alcoholic who started out as my buddy. Clarence was different. He had become comfortable with the mask.

"What's wrong?" He insisted on an answer. Had he failed to notice that we had not had sex in more than a month? He had staked out a sleeping position on the very edge of the bed, with a huge no-person's land in the middle. When I touched him, he flinched and nearly fell off the mattress. In interviews, he insisted that he would always be the first person in his office in the morning and the last to leave at night, and he bragged in speeches about his religiosity. The presence of his son in the apartment eliminated any physical signs of affection between the two of us, pursuant to Clarence's new rules. Surely he realized that he was using

222

religion, his career, his son, and even his running in order to retreat from the relationship? His retreat had worked very well, because I was the master of retreat, myself, and I did not have the ability to fight his. I had a hard enough time fighting my own. Unable to have this conversation with Clarence, I knew what it might lead to, and so we had to engage in a different conversation—a safe one, that allowed Clarence to feel enraged and vengeful, his two familiar default positions.

"It's not working because of my family and my friends," I said. "They listen to the speeches that you give all over the country and they read the newspapers and the magazines that print articles about you, and they all hate what you say. They make fun of you behind your back. When you are with them, you argue all the time now. Your hero is Thomas Sowell, and you talk about libertarians. Nobody has heard of that stuff. You criticize Martin Luther King, Thurgood Marshal, and Jesse Jackson, and you expect the National Bar Association to invite you to speak to them. You even criticize your own sister for being disadvantaged, because you think that white people should not be expected to help us. You act and sound more like your grandfather every day—and he was a horrible man. I just can't take it anymore. And it's just going to get worse. Soon, I will not have any friends left. Nobody I know can stand the positions you take and they all hate the conservatives and religious freaks who are your friends."

He could talk for hours about the issues I raised. I pretended to listen. I had given him others to blame for my decision—the same types who had been "beating up on him" since he left the Hill, since he began campaigning for Republicans. Clarence was not at fault, and there was nothing he could do, except to take revenge on them, to show them all. They would suffer for what they tried to do to him. Didn't he know that, when he flinched or shrugged off my caress, that I could not bring myself to caress him a second time? That when he ignored my question or refused to look at me, I would walk out of the room? Didn't he notice that, when he was making dinner the week before and he gruffly rebuffed my offer of help, that I did not offer again? It would only get worse. I had been there before and I did not want to spend years in a relationship in which I would be angry with the person sleeping next to me—or ignoring him completely.

I knew exactly how I could resurrect the relationship. When he flinched at my touch in bed, I could have gently but persistently caressed him again, accepting the risk that he would have pushed me away or left the bed entirely. If that happened, I might have pouted or cried and then we would have had great make-up sex. When he ignored me, I could have walked closer to him and talked louder to him, accepting the risk that he would have escalated to telling me outright to shut up or leave him alone. If that happened, I might have pouted or cried and then we would have had great make-up sex. When he refused my offer of help in the kitchen, I could have ignored the gruffness and helped anyway, accepting the risk that he would have snatched the spoon or knife from my hand. If that happened, I might have pouted or cried and then we would have had great make-up sex. He might promise to change, and to do better in the future. But that future would never come. I could not see myself in these scenarios, which play out every day in miserable kitchens and bedrooms all over the world. All I could do is what I had done during the past week. I recognized hostility. I retreated to become invisible, part of the wall. I replaced my sentences with grunts. My books replaced my presence. Clarence, deep into his own retreat, had failed to notice mine.

Clarence had to retreat because he was transforming himself, like a snake shedding its skin. His spontaneity, laughter, sexiness, and humanity had been stifled so that he could please the political hacks, evangelicals, conservatives, libertarians, and entertainers, those who would enable him to exact his revenge on the critics who had ridiculed him or attempted to stop the progress of his career. As he was being prepared for the bench or other endeavors, he had to please those who could make that happen. He had to demonstrate his loyalty. Above all, he had to convince them that he would continue to show his appreciation after it happens. Clarence had already evolved into his hate-filled grandfather as a result of the criticism hurled at him by many black writers, groups of professors, and civil-rights leaders. Holding them in contempt, he often used one of his grandfather's favorite sayings to summarize his thoughts about them: "Niggers and flies, I do despise. The more I see Niggers, the more I like flies." As he had changed into his grandfather in private, I must have played the role of Tiny, absorbing the vitriol, tolerating the gruffness, explaining him to others whom he had hurt, and refusing to be offended or to take slights personally. Eventually, I would be a martyr to his whims and to his obsessive quest for revenge, nagging him out of his black moods and entertaining him in a narrow world of his own invention.

In order to accept the risks that a continued relationship with Clarence posed, I would have to be a very different person—more trusting, more forgiving, and more flexible than I am or have ever been. The levels of tolerance, generosity, patience, and good humor that I forced myself to develop were simply not sufficient to sustain a relationship with the new Clarence, who was still complaining about my stupid family and friends and their refusal to understand and appreciate him. I accepted the possibility that Clarence thought I was a shallow, insensitive woman, who abandoned him in his hour of need just because of what others thought of him. But, ever the gentleman, he did not speak these thoughts. His salad remained uneaten. With a mime of writing in the air, I requested the check, which was delivered swiftly to the table. Lifting my right index finger to signal to the server to remain, I counted out cash for him. Then I wolfed down the remaining salad on my plate, stood up, and leaned over to Clarence. "It really is over," I whispered softly in his ear before I walked out of the door into the cool night.

# Scene Thirty-Two

## The Arch

The line inched forward toward the ticket taker, but I was not happy. I looked around at the subterranean room and surveyed the crowd. I was still the only black person in line, and I would be seated soon. It was my third day in Saint Louis, and I had failed to persuade anyone to accept the second ticket that I had purchased the day before for the ride. The hotel I had checked into was across the street from the base of one of the Arch's feet, and the structure drew me like a giant magnet. As I wandered around the grassy park at the base, I saw a knot of tourists emerging from a cleverly concealed door that led to an underground room. It was the entrance to the Saint Louis Arch. Nothing had prepared me for the possibility that the Arch had been designed so that people could travel inside it, stand at an observation window, and then travel down the other side. The viewing platform and window at the apex were cleverly designed so that they could not be seen from the structure's exterior. It seemed a miracle of design to me. It reminded me of the Eiffel Tower. I had been unable to persuade anyone to visit the Tower with me, either, because they all insisted that the crowds would be too huge and that it would be boring. In fact, there had been no line for the elevator to the top of the Eiffel Tower, but I could not tolerate a ride to the apex of that tower. I got out on the second level—still hundreds of feet above the ground—where, strangely enough, a crepe restaurant did a thriving business. The swirls of iron were like lace and I was surrounded on all sides by a miracle of engineering when I stepped onto the Eiffel Tower's platform, which enabled tourists to walk the entire circumference of the edifice. Deathly afraid of heights, I did walk around the platform, making sure I stayed away from the edge.

I was in Saint Louis to attend the National Bar Association Convention, an annual professional-growth and networking gathering of black lawyers and judges. The organization was founded in the early twentieth century because its white counterpart had, since its creation, excluded black lawyers. When I found myself in the area where tickets were being sold for the trip inside the Arch, I was ambivalent. On one hand, I could not resist the pull of the Arch and I felt compelled to experience everything it had to offer. On the other hand, I was still deathly afraid of heights and I was not always able to conquer my fear.

My latest problem had occurred on a ski trip to Pennsylvania about two years earlier. Knowing my problem, I had spent two days falling in mushy snow on the bunny slope. The third day, I was ready to try the beginner's slope, so that I would not be falling in mud. I stood in line to board the ski lift. It was my turn to step into the sling and get propelled into the void, but I could not make my feet move forward. The sight of the flimsy cable and the empty space around it made my stomach turn, and I could not even force myself to walk up the bunny slope the next day. Several years before the ski trip incident was the Brazil incident. That fiasco involved a ferry ride to small rounded mountains rising off the beach in Rio de Janeiro. The twin mountains resemble a pair of women's breasts, and a cable car stretches between the two so that, while traveling from one to the other, riders can view the beach, the city, and the ocean. I made it to the top of the first mountain but, when I looked at the seat I would occupy in the cable car, the cable that stretched out into the sky, and the void that ended in the water, I turned back and nearly collided with the tourists behind me. I fled to the bathroom and threw up until my friends returned from the second mountain.

If I bought two tickets, I thought that, maybe, I could persuade somebody to go up in the Arch with me and, that way, I could force myself to do it. "How many tickets would you like?" asked the acne-scarred teenager as he reached for my twenty-dollar bill. 'Two," I responded confidently. Surely Sid would accept the invitation. After all, he was certainly eager to please me last night. We had traveled to East Saint Louis for a night of fun. My lover for several years, Sid was also easy to please. A short attorney, he was quick to make fun of himself. "My brother says that if they straightened out my bow legs, I would be six-feet tall," he laughed. When he wanted to be romantic, he said he misses me so much that "my dick is harder than the D.C. Bar." He serenaded me with *Wild Thing*.

Our night of fun consisted of visiting strip clubs. Sid had bulging, round eyes like a calf, and a tulip-shaped nose. His lips were full and rubbery and he loved hats, jewelry, and women, and they loved him back. His best feature was his speaking voice, which was perfectly pitched, flexible, and convincing. When he laughed, he threw his head back and stomped his feet. Men also wanted to be around him and he seldom had to buy more than one drink for himself at any bar. Men bought him drinks so that he would continue to tell jokes and to bring women into the group. Women grabbed his behind and surreptitiously passed him their business cards.

I loved the strip clubs more than Sid did. They bored him. To relieve the boredom, Sid decided to convince at least one dancer per club to visit our hotel room after her routine. It had worked in the first three clubs. In the fourth club, Sid was obsessed about buying me a lap dance, which I was not familiar with. Nevertheless, I said, "Wow, that would be great!" Sid knew that I loved women, but he never agreed to a threesome. Instead, he loved to be sucked, and intercourse could last for hours. He ejaculated when he chose to. As soon as we entered the fourth club, Sid started an argument with the dancer on stage. All of the dancers in the club looked eerily similar. Extensive plastic surgery combined with one person's definition of beauty resulted in all the dancers being blonde, in their early twenties, with tiny noses, wide lips, thin bodies, and huge breasts. False eyelashes and gobs of makeup completed the look. "I've never done a woman before," the dancer protested. "I don't know if I could." Sid feigned anger in order to pressure her. This was his idea of a good time.

"Just do what you would do for a man," he insisted. That should be easy. I'll pay whatever you want for the lap dance!" The woman shook her head no as she leaned over the edge of the stage. A dancer clone emerged from stage right. "I've done women's parties before and I've done live acts with women on the stage, too," she bragged. She looked past Sid at me. I was the only woman in the audience. "I'll do a lap dance for her," she said, smiling at me. Then she turned and walked off the stage.

I was mystified. "What does *that* mean?" I asked Sid. "Just be cool and follow her," he said. "She will take us to a private area where the lap dances are done." He rushed to a darkened area. How could I be cool? I had no idea what was going to happen. What is a lap dance? The three of us ended up in a curtained area at the rear of the club where a padded leather chair had been shoved against a wall. "Sit here," Sid whispered. As soon as I sat in the chair, the dancer stood in front of me and straddled my legs. I wore a black silk pant suit that was so thin, the slightest breeze caused it to outline my body like a shadow. The dancer placed her entire upper torso against my chest and I was in heaven. She wore a sequined bra that barely covered her nipples, and a G-string that barely covered her bottom. When she heard me moan, she turned her back to me and lowered her buttocks toward my crotch. Just then, I heard the shuffling of feet that a congregation would make as they approached the altar for Holy Communion.

The entire male audience had arrived to watch. About a dozen men were approaching me from all sides, and their arms were stretched forward like zombies in an effort to touch me anywhere. The rules of lap dance prohibited them from touching the dancer, but those rules evidently did not apply to fellow patrons. Sid's vast experience in strip club matters had not prepared him for this phenomenon. He watched in stunned silence as the closest man stroked my wrist. That broke the spell and Sid woke up. "What the fuck do you think you're doing, motherfucker?" he raged. He actually hissed as he shoved the patron away from me. The man seemed to be in a daze, and he quickly apologized—to Sid, not to me. "I'm sorry, man. I didn't mean to do that," he mumbled. His fellow zombies also began to mumble and shuffle away, but none of them returned to their seats in front of the stage. This show was much better.

Sid continued to curse and shove the men as they forgot themselves and edged closer to my seat in slow motion. The stripper was oblivious, as she undulated onto creases between my legs and shoved her sex onto mine. Her eyes were closed and she seemed to reach orgasm at least three times as she caressed her own body and mine with her fingers and hands. By the time she finished with me, my arms and legs were spread wide and the front of the silk suit had been slimed from the waist to my knees. Even my feet were tingling. Although neither of us had removed any clothing, I felt like I had been naked in bed with her. I had reached orgasm at least six times, in spite of the shadows that Sid had kept at bay. Yes, Sid had aimed to please the night before so, maybe, he would join me for the trip inside the Arch.

I found Sid holding forth in the bar area, regaling the drinkers with a description of his evening heroics. When I interrupted to offer him a ticket, his response was swift. "Honey, there is no way I'm going up in that thing." Nobody else was willing to make the trip, either. I was on my own. The tickets would expire soon, and I ran across the street so that I would not be late. When my turn came to board the cubicle, I first peered inside. It held two rows of three people each, with their knees touching as they faced each other and their thighs pressed against each other on the narrow seats. The metal door slid open and shut with a thud, and the occupants were whisked away en masse. I did not suffer from claustrophobia, and I was happy to see that there was no view of the outside world once the doors slid together. I could do this. I sprang quickly inside and was followed immediately by a family of five, who complained miserably about the oppressive heat. The Arch is not air conditioned. A sucking sound followed the closing of the door, and my ears popped as we were yanked upward. In less than two minutes, the door slid open and I was in hell.

In front of me was a huge, yellow-tinted window that stretched from the floor to the ceiling. It was invisible from the ground because of the color and the curvature of the glass. Outside was a stunning view of the Mississippi River, about twelve western states, and the city of Saint Louis. The crowd of white people pressed their faces against the six-inch-thick, scratched glass and identified the states laid out below them. I could not feel the floor beneath my feet. I was floating and about to crash into the grass at the base of the Arch. I peered at the window from the corner of my eye and tried to calm myself and search for the cubicle that would deliver me from hell. By concentrating on the search as quickly as possible, maybe I could stop myself from throwing up on these people. There was no bathroom available for hiding. I located the first car heading back to Earth just in time.

I headed straight for the bar in the hotel and ordered a Jack Daniels neat to calm my stomach. As I gulped it down, I saw Sid and his buddies walking toward me. "How was the Arch?" he asked, smiling. Was my face green from the ordeal? Was I perspiring? What difference did it make? I set the drink on the bar with nerves of steel. "Too bad you were too much of a chicken to go," I smiled. "It was great. Sorry you missed it, man!" I turned my back to them and finished my whiskey in silence.

# Scene Thirty-Three

Romantic

"This is very romantic, isn't it?" Rich whispered, reaching for the last piece of New York strip steak, medium rare, just like he ordered it. "It certainly is," Gary agreed. I watched Gary swallow a mouthful of my best red wine. Gary had appeared at my house about three hours earlier with his buddy Rich in tow. Although I had never met Rich before, Gary and I had been lovers for about two years. We had been lovers because Gary possessed several endearing attributes, the most obvious of which was his physical beauty. A honey-colored man, he had classic, soft curly light-brown hair that framed slanted eyes, high cheekbones, a tilted nose, and a square jaw. His broad, flat lips smiled perpetually. Broad shoulders tapered to a tiny waist and narrow, rounded hips, and bow legs and a dancer's light step completed the picture. Women of all ages and races admired him on the street, and he was accustomed to feminine attention. He also got feminine attention because he was charming, witty, and friendly. Gary also had a gorgeous, long thin penis with a bulbous head that was rarely soft.

Gary possessed several vices, however. He lived in a hotel suite because he peddled weed to the manager at discount. He loved to gamble, and he won my ten-year-old daughter's heart because he had taught her how to win at and deal blackjack. The card game bored me to tears. Gary drank to excess whenever he could, and he was about to polish off the wine that I had just uncorked at his request. Rich had requested the steak dinner and the candlelight, in my best crystal candelabra. As I smiled at the two men, my thoughts wandered to an experience more than ten years in the past.

In law school, I had taken a lover, Alfred, who thought he was a player. He had soft, long bushy hair and eyebrows so thick that they looked painted onto his high forehead. His eyes were immense and bulging and his lashes were so long and curly that they looked like they belonged on a camel. His skin was brown and freckled, with scars from old fights and weapons. Unlike Gary, Alfred was tall and muscular, with narrow shoulders, high round buttocks and massive thighs. Like Gary, he was accustomed to admiring glances and flirty remarks from women. It had taken many months of experienced seduction for Alfred to persuade me to have sex with him, and this was our very first encounter. After an episode of athletic intercourse, Alfred and I were recovering on the sofa in his apartment when his best friend, George, walked in. I searched for my clothing in embarrassment and both men told me not to bother. Alfred asked George, "Don't you think Lillian is beautiful?" George replied, "Yes, I think Lillian is very beautiful." Then Alfred asked, "Would you like to make love to Lillian?" George replied, "Yes, very much." Walking toward me, he began to strip naked out of his raw silk suit. I, in turn, was amazed at the sophistication and planning that had brought me to the encounter, which I could not have imagined.

Physically, George was the opposite of Alfred. He was short, slight, and almost bony. But, when his penis emerged from his custom-tailored trousers, he proved equally well endowed with his own twelve-inch member. Alfred saw that I was aroused by the sight of George's rampant nudity. "Go ahead, Lillian," he simply said. "I want you to." And so I did, while Alfred watched intently from the sofa, sipping red wine and smoking a joint.

I forced myself to focus on the two men at the dinner table, ten years later. Rich was not nearly as handsome as Gary. His skin coloring, height, and build were all medium, but his ability to convince me to fix a steak dinner, open a bottle of wine, and light candles for the table revealed a knowledge of female thought and behavior that was awe-inspiring. His body language, voice, and vocabulary were utterly seductive. The man oozed great-sexual-experience-on-the-horizon so effectively that my brain was mush. When he whispered, "Do you have any candles?" it sent shivers of anticipation down my spine. Even the sight of his teeth on the forkful of steak was sensuous. I wanted to be that steak.

All three of us stood and pushed our chairs under the table at the same time. Somebody said, "It's getting really late," and I said, "You don't have to go." Gary looked puzzled. "Who doesn't have to go?" he asked. "Nobody has to go," I said. "You can spend the night here." I pointed to the stairs leading to the master bedroom. The three of us ended up naked on the queen-sized bed. Rich had a penis almost exactly like Gary's, except darker, but his ravenous hands and mouth were the perfect combination of gentle and rough. As I rolled over and over between the two men, even while gasping for breath in the midst of several orgasms, I noticed that something was wrong. In the throes of his second orgasm, Rich had reached for Gary's hand and Gary had slapped his hand away for the third time. Rich was clearly bisexual. Was Gary bisexual also? Was this really the first time Rich had made a pass at him? This revelation amused me greatly. Gary spied me giggling and he stormed out of the bedroom in a snit. I laughed even harder. Our wonderful threesome had come to an abrupt end.

# Scene Thirty-Four
## Another Attic

I had to turn around and walk backwards up the steep stairs in order to wrestle the big red suitcase into my room. I regretted buying it. New technology meant that I could have purchased a lighter, stronger, and more maneuverable one. When I banged my elbows against the narrow walls, I did not care what my two condo roommates at the Norman Mailer Writers Colony heard. "Shit!" I muttered. "Fuck!" My heel hit thin air as I reached the floor of the attic. I looked around. "Goddamn it," I thought. "This is what I get for being the last to arrive and choose bedrooms!" I backed into the room and struck my head twice on the sloping ceiling. "Damn!" I looked up at the ceiling. The day before my trip to Provincetown, Massachusetts, I had gotten my grey edges touched up and, now, there were two brown spots on the ceiling to mark the place where I had banged my head.

When the grey hairs had first appeared, I plucked each one out with painstaking care and tweezers. But, at age fifty, there had been so many that I had to choose between baldness or greyness. When I entered the courthouse for a trial one morning at about that time, I struck up a conversation with one of my favorite courtroom clerks. "Hey, Tom," I said. "I always thought grey hair made a man look distinguished. What do you think?" He looked at me. "Yeah," he responded. "That's right." I smiled. "Well," I asked, "what do you think about grey hair for a woman?" He turned and looked me in the face. "Grey hair makes a man look distinguished, but it makes a woman look distraught." I stopped in my tracks as he strode into the courthouse.

I recalled the conversation as I explored the room, banging my head against the sloping ceiling above the collapsible table that sat in front of a window. I put my clothes in the closet and then, while closing the closet door, I banged my head against the ceiling. When I arranged my reading material on the nightstand beside the bed, I bumped my head on the ceiling that sloped above it. Reaching for the pillows, I put the feather one inside the closet, because I am allergic, and that movement resulted in another bump on the closet ceiling. By the time I crawled into bed beneath a skylight an hour later, I counted eight brown spots where my freshly-dyed hair had met the white paint on the ceiling of the cramped space.

When I woke up in the morning, I was in a rage as I got a good look at the irregularly shaped attic space. "How the fuck do they expect me to *write* in a space like this?" I thought, over and over as I added four new brown spots to the collection. I peered into the tiny mirror above a lamp and looked to see whether the white paint had rubbed off onto the sore spots on the top of my head. By the time I reached the Norman Mailer House, across the street on Commercial Avenue, I was in a blinding rage that I found hard to control as I was introduced to my fellow memoir-class students. Sure, the beach and the living room were wonderful, and Kaylie Jones will be a great  instructor, but how the hell was I going to write in a fucking attic?

I was barely listening to the man who led us on the house tour. Finally, I would get to see where my hero, Norman Mailer, had done most of his writing. I had fallen in love with his books at an early age and followed his career as he was interviewed on television, where his great sense of humor never deserted him. I was still shocked by his death, even though it was obvious that he had gotten frail as he aged. Then I noticed we were about to climb a steep set of stairs. They reminded me of the stairs that led to my hated attic bedroom in my parents' home. It was not air-conditioned or heated, the guide  said of Norman Mailer. "Norm continued to climb these stairs to the den even after he began to use two canes. It took him ten minutes to get from the bottom to the top, and you could hear the 'thump, thump' of those canes on the wooden floorboards all through the house in the morning, when he went up and in the evening, when he came back down."

I walked up the stairs to an attic room, where I had to bend my head down to avoid striking it against the ceiling. The room was smaller than my room, which I had just cursed across the street. "And this is where he wrote his last ten books," the guide explained. Even worse, half the space in the room was occupied by an unused piece of gym equipment. "And this machine was installed when Norm decided to exercise," the guide continued. He used it exactly once and never bothered with it again, but it was so awkward to carry up those steep stairs and so difficult to assemble in the heat up here, that they refused to dismantle it and carry it back." A battered wooden desk was shoved against a wall and in front of it was a tattered brown office chair on rollers. On it rested three lumpy cushions. To the right of the desk was a wooden cot, shoved against a sloping wall. A tattered quilt covered half of it. "And this is where Norm napped," the guide pointed.

I was hopeful that I would find one concession to comfort in this cell that had been described as the great writer's study or den. There it was—something in the wall that looked like a dumbwaiter, for the convenient transportation from the downstairs kitchen area of snacks or a cool drink while the great man worked. I did not have a dumbwaiter. The tour was ending. "What is that square recessed area above the bed that appears to be padded?" I asked. "Oh, that," the guide said patiently. "It's actually a window. A pillow has been shoved in it to keep the light out so he could nap." I was the last of the memoir group to descend the steep stairs, and I was ashamed of myself.

# Scene Thirty-Five
## Stress

"The doctor will see you now," announced the perky young receptionist with the perky blonde ponytail, as she interrupted my reading of a transcript. I put away the thick document and grabbed my briefcase for the walk down the inner hallway. Hopefully, this would not take long, since I had scheduled only three hours for sick leave and my obsessive chief judge at the United States Securities and Exchange Commission would surely be noting the time of my return to the office. In spite of my effort to control myself, hope bloomed during the short walk down the corridor. At least I would get answers from the harrowing MRI test, which required my utter immobility while I was surrounded on all sides by a machine that clanged its photographic mission less than an inch from the tip of my nose. Since the neurologist could find no other explanation for the incapacitating headaches—which had confounded my allergist and been impervious to allergy medications and over-the-counter painkillers for three long months—he suspected that a tumor or lesion was lodged in my brain tissue. The pain mystified me and my doctors. It jolted me awake in the middle of the night, yanking me into a sitting position as if I were a puppet and it was the string. It took me a few seconds to figure out why I had been rescued from my recurring nightmare of being chased by some hideous evil monster as I ran through a complex warren of huts and urban ruins, lost and terrified in the inky night, trying to get home.

That morning had been particularly difficult. The pain circled my head like a tight iron band and it radiated down to both shoulders. My temples were sore to the touch and the nightmare had not relinquished its grip on my imagination. The doctor's inner offices were a maze that still confused me, even after several visits for other tests. The perky receptionist led me into the carefully decorated office that had certificates and awards marching across all available wall space. She offered me a seat in the most comfortable leather chair. "The doctor will be in shortly with your test results," she announced proudly before she closed the door soundlessly. I was not prepared for bad news. My life was fine. Mitch would be graduating from college next year, my caseload at the SEC was under control, and I had just bought an uncontested divorce from my second husband, Nero.

Whenever I thought about Nero, a charming, dimpled con artist, I had to laugh. Although he had been a student in a course that I taught at a law school, we had not dated until several years after I resigned from the faculty. He still had not graduated from law school when I married him on a whim, sick with the flu and full of self pity. Three months later, when he enraged me by mentioning my daughter while we were discussing his financial state, I threw him out of my house. We were divorced amicably a few months after that, and we were not friends. Only one part of my life remained a problem for me, and it had nothing to do with my second husband.

The problem was Clarence. I had not escaped the problem by moving out of town for a year shortly after his appointment to the Supreme Court. The confirmation hearing, spread out over several days, had sparked intense interest in Clarence's sex life. When I walked into the courthouse the day after one memorable bit of testimony, a female prosecutor, whom I had known for several years, shouted at me so that about fifty of the hundred or so bystanders could hear her easily. "Lillian," she hollered, "was that your pubic hair in the soda can?" I had to chuckle. "Most likely, it was!" I replied, because everybody who knew the two of us well knew that we had been very close for several years between his marriages.

To my dismay, Clarence's appointment to the Supreme Court did not quell public interest in his personal life. Newspaper reporters did not park themselves outside my house any more, or ring my unlisted telephone number constantly, or visit me at my office any longer, but several publications had mentioned my relationship with Clarence, described me in detail, and linked my name to his without my permission. After I left Clarence, I had moved on from our relationship and I wished him well.

The doctor, an elderly, handsome man with a Santa Claus twinkle and aspect, entered the room and interrupted my assessment of my life. With a flourish, he placed a plastic sheet of x-ray-looking pictures against the beige wall, sat behind his massive maple desk, and began to talk to me.

I heard nothing he said. I was hypnotized by the MRI film, a series of black-and-white images of the interior of my brain tissue. Something about the eight views was terribly wrong, but I could not quite figure out what it was. There were no lumps or holes, but something about the views seemed strange. The doctor pointed at them and raised his voice to get my attention. Reluctantly, I shifted my gaze to his face as he repeated his question. "You know the brain is divided into white matter and grey matter?" I nodded. "You know the white matter transmits signals to the grey matter, which in turn processes those signals?" I nodded. "You see this white matter here?" I nodded. "Notice these spikes in the white matter?" I nodded. "See these spikes in all the views?" I nodded. "These spikes in the white matter are caused by only one condition. Do you know what that is?" I shook my head from side to side, mystified. "These spikes in the white matter result from years of great pain, in your case from migraine headaches. Somehow, until now, you have been able to control your awareness of the pain, but it has been there for many years, doing its damage. Misdiagnosed as sinus headaches, it has been untreated and unmedicated." He looked at me. "Has anyone ever told you that you suffered from migraines?" I shook my head no. "You have atypical migraines, meaning a cause for them has not been determined, and you seem to have no specific trigger for them. You do not have a tumor or lesion, but the brain damage caused by these spikes in the white matter may manifest itself as problems with short-term memory.

Have you experienced short-term memory loss?"

I thought about my recent efforts to describe a friend's eyelashes. "He has eyelashes like a... What do you call that animal with a long neck that has a purple tongue and eats from the tops of trees in the jungle and has orange and white patterns on its fur? Yes, a giraffe! He has eyelashes like a giraffe!" I worried that, before long, I'd be trying to make a remark about something I'd read. I imagined myself saying, "You know, that reminds me of something that I read yesterday in the... What do you call that thing that gets delivered to your door every morning and that you turn the pages and read? Yes, a newspaper! Something I read yesterday in the newspaper..."

The doctor was waiting for my answer. "No," I said. "I have no problem with short-term memory." He looked at me with twinkly pity. "Sometimes," he said, "these migraines are caused by stress. Are you suffering from stress right now?" I thought of the books already written about Clarence, and the ones that would surely be written in the future, and I thought about the friends and strangers who knew intimate details of my long relationship with him. His recent decisions had been a huge disappointment for those who thought he would emulate Thurgood Marshall, the justice whose place he took on the Supreme Court bench. Clarence and I were no longer lovers or friends, but I knew he would continue to avenge himself on those whom he considered to be his enemies. I thought of the retainer that my periodontist had made for me so that I would not continue to wear out my teeth from grinding them in my sleep. "No," I answered. "No, I am not under stress, Doctor." Again, he gave me the twinkle.

I had questions. "Why did my migraines increase in intensity at night, and why did they last for three months with no relief this time?" According to the doctor, the answers were simple. "The migraines are there intermittently during the day and at night," he explained. "Your conscious mind can control your awareness of the pain during the day but, when you are asleep, your unconscious mind lets you feel the pain. As for the intensity of the migraine, the longer it remains untreated, the stronger it becomes. You must stop controlling your awareness of the pain. When it first starts, take a pill. Otherwise, it may be too late. Remember, when you eliminate the pain, you eliminate future damage to the white matter."

Dazed, I left his office. I clutched the film, in a huge manila envelope, and stuffed a prescription for pain pills into my briefcase. I did not have brain cancer, but my life would have to change. The white matter was supposed to be smooth, like a bright ribbon that curved around the dull grey circular masses of brain tissue, but my white matter featured jagged peaks and needles that exploded into the darker circles. I was developing what an older lover called his "CRS—can't remember shit." And I was not even sixty years old.

It was a struggle to get dressed each morning. I had to conquer the nightmares and migraines before I faced myself in the mirror. They also made me dread falling asleep each night. As a result of that reluctance to surrender control, I had been a night owl all my life, and I am a light sleeper. Light and noise often meant I would have a sleepless night because, once awakened, I found it difficult to fall back to sleep. Popping awake at three AM often meant reading in bed until it was time to get dressed for work, and I have been working since I was seventeen. I will retire soon, I decided as I walked out of the lobby into a cloudy afternoon. Then I will write my own book.